Dedication

This book is dedicated to the memory of three men. To David Hare lately of Claygate, Surrey, who is greatly missed. David it was who in overhearing a conversation while pulling a pint for Len Chandler and the author at the Foley Arms, made the observation that his grandfather was at Gallipoli too, and by doing so not only advanced the fellowship of three men whose family histories were touched by the tragedy of 1915, but enhanced the telling of this story. Thank you David.

To the father of the author's grandmother, Sergeant-Major George Ash, 1st Volunteer Battalion and later 5th Reserve Battalion, The Lancashire Fusiliers; previously Colour-Sergeant, 1st Battalion, The Scots Guards and 4th Battalion, The Royal Fusiliers (City of London Regiment) who died in service on 8 March 1915: and also in memory of the brother of the author's grandmother, Private George Vivian Ash, 1st/5th Battalion, The Lancashire Fusiliers, which formed up as part of the 42nd East Lancashire Territorial Division, who was killed in action in the third battle of Krithia, Gallipoli on 4 June 1915, the son of George Ash.

Front Cover: Portrait of Private George Vivian Ash, reproduced by permission of the artist, Mark Adams.

Back Cover. Portrait of Sergeant-Major George Ash, reproduced by permission of the artist, Mark Adams.

FRONTISPIECE

"Sergeant-Major Ash... [has] now left us ... The officers presented ... [him] with a handsome timepiece as a memento of faithful service rendered for many years."

Lancashire Fusiliers' Annual 1907

"An honourable career came to an end with the death of Sergeant-Major Ash on Monday [8 March 1915] ... *The Sergeant-Major was of fine presence - a typical Guardsman in appearance, and in every respect a smart and able soldier. He had the true soldier's respect for the King's Commission, and nothing could exceed the promptness with which he accorded it the full measure of honour. He was ever a courteous and obliging Sergeant-Major ... His return to military duties* [on the outbreak of the Great War in August 1914] *after more than seven years of retirement was probably in accordance with his own wishes as it undoubtedly was in accordance with his sense of duty... The scene at his funeral ... was ... one such as we seldom witness even at interments at which full military honours are accorded."*

Editorial: *Bury Times,* 13 March 1915

"It was with deep regret that we recorded the death of Sergeant-Major Ash. He was a man of wide military experience and one who was held in the highest regard by officers and men of the 1st Volunteer Battalion, the Lancashire Fusiliers, and since his rejoining the force he has earned for himself the same popularity in the Reserve Battalion of the 5th Lancashire Fusiliers Territorials as he enjoyed with the Volunteers. Sergeant-Major Ash was a soldier, and this simple definition possesses a wealth of meaning. He knew his work; he had a capacity for creating the best spirit among the mess, for had he occasion to be displeased he never showed any deep feeling of vexation. He had seen service in Egypt, but Egyptian life had no great attraction for him, as the climate was so intensely hot in the summer months."

Editorial: Bury Guardian, 13 March 1915

Portrait of Sergeant Major George Ash by Mark Adams (Courtesy of the artist)

CONTENTS   Page

v

Acknowledgments

I am indebted to many people in the preparation of this book. If Len Chandler at the Foley Arms in Claygate, Surrey hadn't engaged me in earnest conversation when I first mentioned Gallipoli, and then if he had not set me on a sure course to start the research, this story would never had emerged. If Douglas Warwick hadn't encouraged me, the story might never have been written down in a disciplined way and turned into a book. David Hare soon emerged as a fellow traveller; his Brigadier-General grandfather had served in Gallipoli and my story is enriched by his allowing me to have access to Sir Steuart Hare's diary and, kindly, allowing me to publish extracts from it. Between the time I finished writing and this book emerging in print, David succumbed to cancer. To these and my other friends at the Foley Arms, I say thank you; to the first group for the Gallipoli conversations over the eight months which this story took to emerge and to be written down; to the second group I say thank you for your forbearance over our having hijacked the conversation at times.

My wife was very patient with me when our dining room table disappeared under paper for long periods of time as I wrote the story while hearing the wistful chimes of the *"handsome timepiece"*. She was too late in her warning not to allow the project to take over my life: it did and there is nothing I would rather have done with that part of my life.

As a group before the investigation that led to this book, I have never been particularly aware of archivists. I am now, and I salute their patient dedication and their knowledge. I am grateful to the staff at the Public Record Office in Kew, at the reference library in Bury, the British Library, the Bury Archive Service, the North West Film Archive at Manchester Metropolitan University and Dorset Record Office. All those mentioned have more or less adequate or proper funding. From the museum of the Lancashire Fusiliers in Bury I found treasure too, but their meagre funding is at the opposite end of the scale. I am very grateful to Tony Sprason, the Custodian for his help early on, in uncovering key facts of the story, not least in his care later on in assisting the artist, Mark Adams, with the correct uniforms and insignia for the portraits of Sergeant-Major Ash and his son, Private George Vivian Ash. Without the help of Terry Morgan at the *Bury Times* it might not have been possible to locate the film of the Sergeant-Major's funeral. I am grateful to him for that and his other cheerful acts of helpfulness. Pat Gareipy from the USA gave me some facts about the circumstances of Private Ash's death and its being reported in Bury, which added colour to the account. To the officers and members of the Gallipoli Association I express my thanks for your existence and the mutual interest and fellowship, which we now share.

I am grateful to the *Bury Times* for their permission to reproduce material from the paper.

Jan Griffiths typed the manuscripts and retyped them with skill, speed and cheerfulness while at the same time attending to her *proper* job. It is impossible to imagine how this work would have emerged without her efforts.

My greatest thanks are to the officers of the 1st Volunteer Battalion, the Lancashire Fusiliers, who, when presenting his retirement present to my great grandfather, had it inscribed. The inscription was the golden key to unlocking this story, which I have been compelled to write. I had intended to call the book *"A Handsome Timepiece"* it would have been a worthy title. After I finished writing I visited Gallipoli. The title 'Where *is* Gallipoli?' was inspired by the pathos of those hundreds of Bury boys, all previously part time Territorials of whom their country had no right to expect overseas service, but who nevertheless volunteered to a man. When the Territorials were in Egypt and it became clear they were to reinforce the failing invasion, Vivian Ash and his chums in the ranks may well have intoned: 'Where *is* Gallipoli?' Many a man with a better education than those Bury boys would have asked the same question!

WHERE *IS* GALLIPOLI?

FOREWORD

BY: COLONEL MICHAEL HICKEY (Author of *Gallipoli*)

In thousands of homes across the land there must be fading sepia photographs of young men clad in the drab uniforms of the Great War. One suspects that in the majority of cases a later generation barely gives them a second look; perhaps an elderly relative can tell them something: "That's your great grandfather. He was killed out east - a place called Gallipoli, I think." If gifted with a sense of mild curiosity the young descendant might ask where Gallipoli is, to be given a vague answer, for very few seem to remember that it is in Turkish Thrace, across a narrow strip of water from ancient Troy, and that over twenty thousand Britons never returned from the savage campaign fought there in 1915. Another generation and the photo will be binned, its subject utterly forgotten.

The author of this book, however, is possessed of much more than a sense of mild curiosity, for his fascination with a family heirloom - a "handsome timepiece" - inscribed by the officers of the 1st Volunteer Battalion of the Lancashire Fusiliers in honour of the retirement of Sergeant-Major Ash in 1907, led to the discovery of a lost story. The Sergeant-Major was the author's great grandfather - this much he knew - but by tracing the Sergeant-Major's career in a remarkable feat of detection he unearthed a rich hoard of family and military history, including a cinema film of the man's funeral - the existence of which there was no living knowledge.

George Ash had been born in Dorset and would have spent a life of grinding anonymity as a farm labourer had he not enlisted in the Scots Guards. Warming to the life he gained rapid promotion, transferring to the Royal Fusiliers and finally to the Lancashire Fusiliers where he completed his colour service with the Volunteers as they became part of the new Territorial Force in 1907. He married and fathered a family; took up Bury as the family home, and a son served in the Territorials for a time. In August 1914, the son rejoined the Territorials, volunteering for foreign service; we can imagine Private Ash and his chums asking "Where *is* Gallipoli?" as they left Cairo to reinforce the landings. His father rejoined the colours at the age of 55 for home service. All this information was painstakingly delved from the National Archive at Kew, the Commonwealth War Graves Commission and from the Lancashire Fusiliers' own archive at Bury. By now the author had become aware of the son, who tragically died at Gallipoli where the regular and Territorial Fusiliers suffered appalling losses, plunging the town of Bury into mourning. The old Sergeant-Major never had to mourn his son, for he had died earlier in the same year. A local notable, his funeral was attended by thousands. Of his son the surviving siblings and womenfolk of the family never spoke, muted in their grief; and if the young man had written any letters from Gallipoli they were either destroyed or lost; nothing except the "handsome time-piece" remained.

The author, therefore, had to pick up a cold trail; but his enthusiasm and persistence - aided as he acknowledges by his friends at their local pub - the Foley Arms in Claygate, Surrey, have been rewarded. Using a variety of sources he has been able to reconstruct the civilian and military world in which father and son grew up and lived their lives and has succeeded in bringing both vividly to life. This is social history at its most vital and an important contribution to our knowledge of a world which vanished in four terrible years.

PREFACE

When this story began I used to say to people that I had started on an investigation of some of my forebears which has revealed some very unexpected facts and that the story was going forward in an unpredictable way to a destination of which I could not conceive. So it turned out. This account is part autobiographical and part biographic which makes it difficult to characterise; but there is no fiction in it. Here is the story of how I came to discover the lives of two of my grandmother's closest relatives - her father and her brother both of whom were soldiers with the Lancashire Fusiliers; both of whom died during the Great War. The story grew from my inheritance of a clock, early in 2001, which had been given to my great grandfather in 1907 when he retired from the Army. At that stage I knew nothing that you would call facts about him other than those recorded on the inscription on the clock. Scant as they were, they were enough to open up a trail which allowed me to discover large tracts of the story of his life from his birth into a peasant family in Dorset in 1858, his thirty one years of soldiering in, successively, three crack regiments, the Scots Guards, the Royal Fusiliers and ultimately as a Sergeant-Major in the Lancashire Fusiliers.

Although I knew from my childhood that the Sergeant-Major was held in the highest esteem by his family there was a void as far as his son was concerned. Something dark surrounded the subject of his son, not that he was ever mentioned. There were no men in my grandmother's family at least not during my lifetime. Soldiering was never discussed. The void was glossed over. Occasionally, when scolding me, my grandmother would spit the words *"the Dardanelles"* in rebuke as if I was in some way unworthy. Her voice would break with emotion. I would make myself scarce. The subject was not so much dropped, it was only an allusion anyway, and it was never developed. The reader may find it unexpected that a man should arrive in his 59th year and not know that his grandmother's brother died at Gallipoli. A campaign of infamy, of death and suffering on a shocking scale, of heroism, valour, bad leadership and unmitigated (except in the withdrawal) defeat for the British Army. A campaign in which the Lancashire Fusiliers fought gloriously, as did others, but whose losses ripped the heart out of the town of Bury, their home and my grandparents home. Bury bled.

If the readers can comprehend that I was in ignorance of all this in spite of being a frequent visitor to the town for the first 16 years of my life, they will understand my need to find out why Gallipoli happened and to write it down. This is not a book about the Gallipoli campaign; I touch only briefly on the land battles there. It is a book about how I came to find out about the secrets of my soldier forebears which, I assert, were deliberately kept from me, perhaps not in an organised conspiracy but as a subliminal part of my grandmother's strategy for coping with the loss of her brother. Her determination to shut out the past (while living in a town which marked Gallipoli Sunday every year for the rest of her life from its first anniversary in 1916, and which continues to this day) is matched only by my determination to learn how that great tragedy, which robbed Bury of her poor boys, came to happen.

Claygate 4 December 2001

Chapter 1

The Inheritance

It all started with a clock. I have known Sergeant-Major Ash's clock practically all my life. From my first senses as a child, and long before I knew what *'esteem'* was, I knew that my mother's family held Sergeant-Major Ash high in it. But, if it hadn't been for his clock and the inscription on that clock, and indeed a chance conversation in the local pub, this story would never have been told. It would not be true to say that the memory of the Sergeant-Major *might* have slipped into oblivion and lain there undisturbed until the end of time. The fact is that until I inherited the clock late in the year 2000 the memory of him being talked about had already become dormant. If providence had determined that his memory should have been forgotten forever that would have been a travesty, as this story will show.

Sergeant-Major Ash was my grandmother's father. I never knew him, naturally, but he was one of those success symbols, which a working class family elevates into a position from where glory can be reflected. Although he started life as a simple farm labourer, he was, by the standards of working class folk in the second half of the 19th and early 20th century, a very successful man. Having had a long career as a non-commissioned officer (as I was to discover) he fully justified the esteem in which he was held by his family and indeed by his men, his fellow NCOs, his officers and the local community in which he spent the last 19 years of his life. Little did I realise the extent to which he had established himself as a popular and successful character in his adoptive town of Bury in Lancashire. But I knew nothing of the extent of this. For my part I only perceived this reflected glory by radiation to me from my grandmother, which was casually absorbed with only subliminal sub-conscious awareness. It was to my grandmother, known always to her peers as 'Cissie', and my mother, who died respectively in 1964 and 1977, that I owe such memories about Sergeant-Major Ash that I retain. My mother was only four years old when grandfather Ash died so she must have absorbed well from her mother and her aunts the esteem in which he was held.

I never heard my mother speak of Gallipoli or the Dardanelles. Why would she you may ask? In any event, being born in 1910 she was too young to have any substantive memories of the Great War. Being, as I am, a child of the Second World War, all references to "the war" when I was a youngster were to that war from which the parents of my generation had just emerged, intact if they were lucky. Rationing seemed to be the chief topic of conversation. Every generation has its heroes I suppose, but in later life I have come to realise what heroes those mums were who raised their families in the face of bombing and the sinister threats of the tyrant dictators. The "Great War" as I have come to call it, didn't seem to be mentioned much in our house. Our parents, as I have said, were too young to have been much touched by it. It was only in later years of my life that I started hearing about things like "the first day of the Somme" or "Ypres" or "Vimy Ridge" and began to realise that, awful though the Second World War had been for those who had had to fight it or suffer it on the Home Front, it was nothing compared with the slaughter, the suffering, and the waste which had been the hard lot of the citizen armies which fought the Great War. My mother's parents were old enough to have lived through the Great War in their early married lives, as had mine in the second, but still the topic did not seem to come up in conversation. But occasionally, just very occasionally, my grandmother would refer to the Dardanelles; no context for this was ever apparent to me. But whenever she did make reference to it, it was with an intense bitterness, which a child could understand but not describe.

Perhaps it was the way she spat the word *"Dardanelles"*. The provocation for this bitter reference, as I realise now with the benefit of more worldly experience, came only when as a child I had overstepped the mark in some way; in other words it seemed as if it was uttered as part of a rebuke. It was definitely not referred to as a way of handing down knowledge. With adult antennae you might perhaps think that it was a way of me being labelled "unworthy"; I am certain about this - there was no mistaking it. There was no mistaking the bitterness in her heart and the quiver in her voice as she came close to tears. Of course I knew nothing at the time of why she held the name in such contempt. I fear I continued to know next to nothing about the horror of the Dardanelles campaign until after she was dead. I simply knew it was a bad news subject and was best avoided. There it would have lain, unremembered, unlamented, as I have noted, were it not for the clock. The memory of the Sergeant-Major would have faded long ago and Gallipoli and the Dardanelles campaign would have no particular significance for me.

The "handsome timepiece" presented to Sgt-Major George Ash on his retirement from the Lancashire Fusiliers in 1907, inherited by his grandson (the author) in 2001. The inscription in the clock allowed the story of "Where *Is* Gallipoli? to be discovered.

(Author's photo)

In a history of The Lancashire Fusiliers* is told how in 1891 was founded *The Lancashire Fusiliers Annual* and which was to be published annually and continuously until 1926. These Annuals, in the words of the history, *"constitute an invaluable record...."*; they do indeed and my story and my discoveries would have been the poorer without them. It would not be going too far to assert that the story may never have emerged at all without *The Lancashire Fusiliers Annual!* In the words used at the time of its conception the object of the Annual was *"primarily to furnish a permanent and authentic record of the work of each battalion for the year, together with information as to Regimental matters, amusements, camps of instruction, rifle competitions and such other items as may be communicated to the editors by each battalion; and secondarily to be a vehicle for recording and circulating papers on historical...subjects, ... which are likely to be useful..."*

As I was to find out shortly after this story began, in *The Lancashire Fusiliers' Annual* dated 31st December 1907, under the heading of *'1st Volunteer Battalion'* is contained the following note: *"Sergeant-Major Ash and Colour-Sergeant Hickie* [of whom we will hear again] *have now left us. The officers presented each of them with a handsome timepiece as a memento of faithful service rendered for many years."* It is indeed a handsome timepiece. I know because it has pride of place as it tick-tocks in my dining room and I hear it as I write these words. It is, apparently, not particularly valuable in the market. No matter, it looks and sounds fine and as with many an heirloom, there is no sensible price at which I would part with it.

The clock is a black marble mantle clock with a French movement standing 18" high and 11" across. It has a bevelled glass case front and back revealing a mercury pendulum, which swings to and fro at its regular beat of 120 movements per minute. It is a clock with character; its personality and its gentle tick-tock engages you and makes a statement announcing its presence when you enter its place.

When I first saw this clock I can't say. This is simply because it is like asking when did you first see your grandparents. My grandmother (or "Cissie" as she was called by all her siblings and peers for reasons not understood by me) kept the clock in the front parlour of the back to back house in which she lived along with my grandpa Harry Barlow at 36 Grosvenor Street, Bury, Lancashire.

Even as a child, with no yet developed taste, it made a commanding statement on making its acquaintance; it announced itself with its presence! Grosvenor Street (and indeed Bury itself) was a different world to that which was normal for me as a child. Visiting my grandparents' house there, first from York and later from Guildford in Surrey, brought me in touch with working class housing, cobbled streets, trams and smoke-grimed buildings. In the 1940s and 1950s Bury was still a cotton town, perhaps not prosperous but still completely connected with its industrial past.

---

*A Short History of XX [regimental shorthand for the 20th Regiment of Foot-raised in 1688] the Lancashire Fusiliers: by Major-General G Surtees, CB, CBE, MC, Colonel, XX The Lancashire Fusiliers: 1955

Grosvenor Street, Bury -
A photo from the 1960s
(Courtesy Bury Library)

As was commonplace among working class families, the front parlour at 36, Grosvenor Street, Bury was for visitors use only. The clock stood proudly on the sideboard. Being family, we never sat in the parlour. The dining room was where the whole of life went by, with the scullery off it and the back yard off that. All approaches to the house, all deliveries seemed to come from the narrow cobbled street, which connected the backs of the terraced houses. The front of the house and the front parlour were a foreign land. Even if I had never been sent into that hallowed room to fetch the biscuit barrel, as I often was, I would still remember that clock as one of my earliest childhood memories. I remember on stop-over visits, lying sleepless in bed hearing many unfamiliar noises. The goods yard, a few hundred yards away, assaulted the ear every few minutes or so with the strange, to me at the time and now extinct, long stereophonic scale of the clangs of buffer on buffer as the goods wagons were shunted to and fro to be made into trains. I remember that seemingly relentless night-long procession of metallic noise and how I cursed it. But how soothing was the sound of the clock (I didn't know at first that it was Sergeant-Major Ash's clock) as it struck the half hour and the hour (counting the strikes was then, as it still is now, compulsive). How familiar that strike was to become as I lay awake, giving as it did a feeling of security in an otherwise strange place.

As already mentioned, the clock now sits in my dining room. For years and years, before I inherited it, it never worked. On taking possession my first act was to have it seen to by a skilled horologist. His verdict was that there was nothing much wrong with it. The prognosis was that if the clock were not disturbed (which might disbalance the mechanism through excessive or unnatural pendulum movement) it would run and run. So, in January 2001 it took up its position, restored, working and fully deserving the description of a *"handsome timepiece"* given to it (as I had discovered) in the 1907 Lancashire Fusiliers' Annual.

When it first stood in my dining room, after I had set it running following its collection from the horologist, my first thought was to admire how "handsome" it is and how well it sits in my Edwardian home. It was obviously not long before it chimed the hour. At that moment my mind flew straight to my childhood, to black puddings, the muffin man calling from the street and the shunting of trains. It was the same chime, yes, I remembered the chime from the front parlour in 36 Grosvenor Street, Bury; the same chime I remembered as I lay awake in bed and which provided me with such comfort from the unwelcome noise of the shunting.

I have often debated with myself and others the issue of how reliable memories are - certainly, the memory is fickle and capricious and I wonder if it is vulnerable to conditioning over time, so that one ends up remembering something one's mind has become used to and comfortable with but which has in fact evolved from a modified memory, a memory of a remembered memory! It is easy to have a foot in both camps on this one. Sometimes, the memory when faced with the incontrovertible is proved wrong or exaggerated, sometimes, however, it can be proved right, lighthouse true after decades. This story unfolded from a few scraps of memory, of which more later, some of which proved to be unfailing beacon lights. Before discussing that, however, I claim the childhood memory of the chime of the *"handsome timepiece"* . On this, at least, I cannot be gainsaid.

My grandmother Cissie, being as I was later to find out, the oldest surviving child of the Sergeant-Major, presumably inherited the clock on the death of her mother, the Sergeant-Major's wife whom I discovered later died in 1929. When I first became aware of the clock in the 1940's, so far as I knew it had always been in Grosvenor Street, Bury. As I was to find out, the clock had been in two pubs - The Grey Mare Hotel in Bury and the Nob Inn in Little Lever a few miles from Bury, where George Ash had been for a while the licensee - as well as at 8, School Brow, Bury where he lived for a while, and in fact he died and where his widow continued to live until her death in 1929. All this I had to discover - so far as I knew until 2001 the clock was always from Grosvenor Street.

The Grey Mare Hotel, Bury -
A photo from the 1960s.
(Courtesy of Bury Library)

School Brow, Bury, where Sergeant-Major Ash died on 8 March 1915 and where his widow continued to live until her death in August 1929.
(Courtesy of Bury Library)

When my grandparents moved to Wimbledon in 1958 the clock came with them. When they became old and frail their home was broken up and the clock moved with them to my parents' home, in Hinchley Wood, Esher, Surrey. After Cissie's death in 1965 my mother inherited the clock and it moved with them to Cobham, Surrey in 1968. When my mother died in 1977 my father inherited the clock. During its long years in Cobham the clock did not run reliably, and when my father's home was broken up in 2000 the clock had not worked for years in spite of efforts to have it repaired. Happily for me, my brother was less interested in the clock than me and my interest in it then was solely because the *handsome time-piece* from the Edwardian era would sit comfortably in my own Edwardian family home. My step-mother gave me the clock and so it arrived in its new home in Claygate, Surrey after its visit to the horologist.

Soon after the clock arrived, but while I was still in the habit of entering the dining room with the sole purpose of gazing at it, I began to get more and more intrigued by the inscribed dedication on it:-

> **"PRESENTED TO SERGEANT-MAJOR G ASH**
> **AFTER 13 YEARS FAITHFUL SERVICE, BY THE OFFICERS**
> **of the**
> **1st VOLUNTEER BATTALION LANCASHIRE FUSILIERS,**
> **OCTOBER 1907"**

I found myself looking more and more at this inscription. It began to pro-voke my interest. What lay behind it? Who was this man whose clock I was now enjoying? What had he done with his life? The inscription and my childhood memories of the 1940s and 1950s were all I had to go on if I were to pursue my curiosity. To say that it was a challenge would be an understatement and left entirely to myself I may never have crossed the start line to use an unfamiliar (to me) military term. As it happened, and entirely through serendipity, I was to get both encouragement and guidance from a very pleasant source.

This part of the story proves how, in the affairs of men (and women) conversation can lead to both stimulation and fruitful incremental knowledge. When my son left the UK to work in the sunshine state, California, he took a long time to settle down. What he missed most he told us was 'the pub'. We have, in Claygate, Surrey, a charming village pub, which it is impossible to visit with any frequency without engaging in pleasant conversation. It is one of those pubs which every village seemed to have in the past, but now, sadly, are fewer and fewer because simple plain values have been pushed out by corporatism or whatever it is! The pub, the Foley Arms, dates back, like my own house, to the late Victorian/Edwardian eras of expansion and development of Claygate, which followed the opening of the railway to London. It is one of those rare pubs that retains its public bar - this is probably why it is good. It has, according to some of its long term regulars, been through a period of *"the Dark Ages"* but today it is on an upswing. Visitors at lunchtime may now even hear of "Gallipoli" as a topic of conversation. This is a new development. It's all part of the story.

In the Foley Arms I have met many interesting people all of whom have some life experience from which it is impossible not to be enriched by the re-telling. Among these pleasant souls are Len Chandler and Douglas Warwick, both former professional soldiers, and both in their very different ways responsible for the effort, which I was encouraged to put into the research that led to this story. Len Chandler is responsible for encouraging me to start the research and I will always be grateful to him for that. Douglas Warwick gave me the prompt to write the story down.

Douglas, having taken an interest in and read some of my minor monographs, gave me the encouragement to take on something bigger. Len Chandler, as it was to emerge, was a fellow traveller, in the sense of having a Gallipoli connection, as indeed was David Hare (an occasional pint puller at the Foley Arms).

A chance remark in the Foley Arms one lunchtime sparked things off. Early in March 2000, when the flush of *the handsome timepiece* inheritance was still aglow, I mentioned it to Len, and my memory, so I thought, that all of Sergeant-Major Ash's sons died in the Great War, at Gallipoli I thought. That was the spark. Len's dad, Private Frederick Chandler, had been wounded at Gallipoli, but had survived. As Len and I were talking about this in the bar, David Hare announced, as he pulled a pint, that his grandfather had commanded the Fusilier Brigade (the 86th) at the Helles landings at Gallipoli. Later I was to confirm that my grandmother's brother had indeed died at Gallipoli. The connection between our ancestors' lives had been revealed from a chance remark, and had escalated and intrigued us in quick time. It was only days before Len's scrap books emerged. Len was surefooted in his advice to me when I told him I wanted to find out more, and in this I owe him much. *"Write"*, he said *"to the Lancashire Fusiliers' Museum, tell them what you know and ask them what they know."*

That same week I wrote. Apart from the inscription I had only a few memories to go on. I tested these memories with my elder brother. Without giving him any prompts in the hope of objective and spontaneous memory recall I asked him what he could remember. Surprisingly, he wasn't able to offer anything, at least not at the time, so I wrote off to the Lancashire Fusiliers' Museum with such facts as I had and a handful of memories, which might or might not be reliable.

The only thing I knew for certain was that Sergeant-Major Ash had served for 13 years until 1907 with the Lancashire Fusiliers. For this I had the primary evidence of the inscription on the clock. I had no other hard evidence, only some fragments of memories. I thought I remembered my grandmother telling me that she had been born in the Tower of London (which is not something which is easy to make up and even less easy to forget) while her father was on garrison duty. Of course I remembered the bitterness as she spat the words *"the Dardanelles"** usually when I had shown some childlike cockiness or insolence. I remembered too that the Ash family seemed to consist only of women. Apart from my grandpa there were no men on my mother's side of the family. I remembered too being told that my grandmother had had, as a 21st birthday treat, a trip to South Africa. In 1906, as it would have been, that would have been quite something! This made me speculate that perhaps her dad had served in the Boer War. But all this was uncorroborated speculation or fallible memory. Soon I would be gathering facts at a pace that was to astonish me. I had started on a quest for knowledge about my ancestry - a mission that was to take me back to Bury, to London, Dorset, and one day will take me to Gallipoli, and it all started with a clock!

The Dardanelles is of course, the name of the straits separating European Turkey from Asian and it was the control over these waters that was the strategic imperative of the campaign. For the most part, apart from feints, the land fighting took place on the European side of the Straits on the Gallipoli peninsular. For my grandmother, it was *the Dardanelles* she spoke of, not *Gallipoli*! I don't know why.

Chapter 2

Gathering Speed

The first and immediate response from the Lancashire Fusiliers' Museum threw one of my scraps of memory into confusion. The Museum Custodian, Mr. Tony Sprason, was puzzled by the reference to the Tower of London (where I thought my grandmother had been born) because, he said with authority, "The Lancashire Fusiliers had never been in garrison there", it being the role of the Royal Fusiliers! To help in his research he asked if I knew the Sergeant-Major's Christian name and where he was born. Such was the paucity of my knowledge that I did not know his Christian name! As to where he lived I had always assumed he was a Bury man but I had to concede that, in fact, I had no evidence at all to support the assumption; and to remind the reader the only evidence I did have was the evidence of the inscription on the clock. On thinking about this again and logically it became clear that there was an unexplained gap.

Sergeant-Major Ash retired in 1907 (I didn't know at what age) *"after 13 years faithful service"*, by a simple deduction he must have joined the Lancashire Fusiliers in 1894. If my grandmother was born in 1884 or 1885 as I thought, then if he was in garrison at the Tower of London he must have had some Army service before 1894. It wasn't to be long before I discovered just how much Army service there had been before 1894!

While I was conjecturing still about this, I heard again in definitive terms from Tony Sprason, the Museum Custodian. As we have already seen from the previous chapter, Tony Sprason had found the reference in the Lancashire Fusiliers' Annual to a *'handsome timepiece'* being presented in 1907 to both Sergeant-Major Ash and Colour-Sergeant Hickie. Joyous though this revelation was, there were several other references to the Sergeant-Major (and to Colour-Sergeant Hickie too).

In his 1906 report, the officer commanding the 1st Volunteer Battalion, the Lancashire Fusiliers, Colonel George E Wike (who I was to discover was to be wounded at Gallipoli) wrote:-

"I cannot close this report without expressing my regret, which will, I know be shared by all the members of the Battalion, that on March 30th we shall lose Sergeant-Major Ash and Sergeant Hickie. We have been singularly fortunate in being associated with Sergeant-Major Ash, who came from the 4th Battalion, Royal Fusiliers, but he had previously been Colour Sergeant in the 1st Battalion, Scots Guards. He has at all times been a smart soldier, intelligent, and most willing to do all he could for the corps. He carries away with him the respect of all - these are not idle words, they are meant. Sergeant Hickie, at Heywood, had stood well and honestly by the two Heywood Companies, and

well he has served the Battalion. We shall always look back with pleasure to our associa-tion with Sergeant Hickie."

So the Sergeant-Major had indeed seen earlier service with the Royal Fusiliers (supporting the Tower of London memory) and before that, which was new and very curious, the Scots Guards.

The Sergeant-Major and Colour-Sergeant Hickie had obviously been close collaborators in the battalion and typically the Colonel's annual report finishes with references such as: *"At Bury Sergeant-Major Ash and at Heywood* [a small town near Bury] *Colour-Sergeant Hickie, both work hard for the corps."*

The 1904 Lancashire Fusiliers' Annual records that: *"We sent to the tournament at Manchester to compete in the bayonet exercise, a team of 16 men and one NCO, and were successful in carrying off the second prize of five guineas. The team was well coached by Sergeant-Major Ash."* The subject of bayonet drill and fighting, and dying by this weapon will come up again in later chapters.

In 1899 we read that, following a musketry competition: *"Sergeant-Major Ash is the best shot in the Battalion, with a record score."* This prompted my brother to recall a delightful story he says was told to us as children, but I can't remember it myself! Evidently, one day at the abattoir in Bury, a bull that had presumably sensed its doom, escaped and was raging free round the market place, which was next door. As can be easily imagined this bull, which wanted nothing more than its life, was causing much consternation and fear. The story goes that Sergeant-Major Ash, who as I have related was *"the best shot in the Battalion"* was called for and he duly shot the bull dead in the street. *

All that is left of Wellington Barracks, Bolton Road, Bury, with the war memorial by Lutyens in the style of The Cenotaph, in the foreground.
(Author's photo, 2003)

Everything that had been revealed by the Lancashire Fusiliers' Annual gave new and intriguing information about Sergeant-Major Ash but it told us nothing of what became of him after his Army service and only the barest outline of his previous service with the Scots Guards and the Royal Fusiliers. I had learnt nothing about any of his sons. Tony Sprason, the Museum Custodian, sent me

---

*Not knowing a date for this event I have found it very difficult to confirm this anecdote through press reports but it remains plausible enough in view of his attested marksmanship.

print-outs from the 'Soldiers Died' CD Rom, but without knowledge of Christian names (which I still lacked) this was not much more than just a list and not at all conclusive.

The 'Soldiers Died' list told me that there were four Ash's who served in the Lancashire Fusiliers and died in the Great War. There was a George Ash who was born in Dorchester and a George Vivian who was born in Chelsea, both of whom enlisted at Bury. One of these (George Vivian) died at Gallipoli. The total number of Ash's died in the Great War was 93. I didn't have enough information to home in on any of these which might have been my relations.

I was very pleased and encouraged by the revelations from the Lancashire Fusiliers' Museum and the new information gained from that source. I needed more, however, so I made my first visit to the Public Record Office in Kew where I was able to examine the original documents in both cases, of the army records of the Attestation and Discharge of Sergeant-Major George Ash. From these I was informed, for the first time that his Christian name was George!

These original documents, some nearly 130 years old, supplied exciting and previously wholly unknown facts. Sergeant-Major Ash was discharged from the Army on 31 March 1907 in consequence of *'having claimed it after three months notice'*. His conduct was described as 'exemplary' he having been awarded six good conduct badges including the Egyptian Medal where he served in the 1882 campaign and the Khedive's Bronze Star, also 1882. On his discharge he had completed 31 years and 231 days service. His intended place of residence was noted quaintly as 'The Grey Mare Hotel', Bury, where he was to become the licensee, as it emerged later.

As noted earlier, I had never heard as a child of any service other than with the Lancashire Fusiliers although, as it turns out, he served with other regiments for longer. I was astonished to discover that he enlisted (as a labourer at the *'apparent'* age of 18) on 11 August 1875 in Dorchester (having been born some 10 miles away in Sydling St Nicholas). My brother and I had always assumed that the family came from Bury. It now rather appeared that they went to Bury in order for Colour-Sergeant Ash (as he then was) to join the Lancashire Fusiliers. Anyway, from later evidence I have established that he was born in 1858, the son of Robert and Jane Ash of Sydling St Nicholas, Dorset.

Bury - a product of the Industrial Revolution. This scene is approximately the view from School Brow, probably taken in the 1940s or 50s
(Courtesy of Bury Library)

What was puzzling, at least to me, was how he came to enlist in the Scots Fusilier Guards* (which is now the Scots Guards) in Dorchester, a quintessentially English town almost as far away from Scotland as you can get! What I have discovered since is that the Scots Guards are not as Scottish as they sound. Their depot is in London at Birdcage Walk and their only presence in Scotland is a recruiting office in Edinburgh Castle.

The scenario in 1875 when George Ash joined up was, I surmise, that a recruiting sergeant turned up in Dorchester and, needing numbers at that time to fill the ranks of the Scots Guards, found a likely lad to be pointed in that direction. Anyway, however it came about, that's what he did and he served with the Scots Fusilier Guards until, on 31 December 1886, he transferred to the 4th Battalion, Royal Fusiliers.

This does nothing to solve the Tower of London mystery and my grandmother's birth there. I established from Sergeant-Major George Ash"s service records that my grandmother, Griselda Ash, was born on 7 November 1885, at a time when her father was still to be with the Scots Fusilier Guards for a further 14 months; this conundrum left me to consider whether that regiment was ever in garrison at The Tower of London, to explain her birth there in 1885. Having had my faith in my memory reinforced (at least in part) I had to believe there was to be an explanation for this apparent mis-match.

> The Tower of London, where George Ash served with the Royal Fusiliers, and the author's great aunt was born.

---

*This regiment was raised in 1642 under the Marquis of Argyle as the Scottish Foot Guards. In 1713 it became known as the Third Guards and as the Scots Fusilier Guards in 1831. It became the Scots Guards in 1877, just after Sergeant-Major Ash joined.

The Sergeant-Major's service record shows his promotion in the Scots Guards as follows:

18 April 1877	- Lance Corporal
23 September 1877	- Corporal
28 September 1880	- Lance Sergeant
28 September 1882	- Sergeant
27 July 1884	- Colour-Sergeant

This suggests that he was Colour-Sergeant throughout his later service with the 4th Battalion Royal Fusiliers from 31 December 1886 to 21 March 1894 when he transferred as Sergeant-Major to the Lancashire Fusiliers. He married Miss Elizabeth Ewen on 17 March 1883 shortly after returning from Egypt on 14 November 1882; she is shown as being 'with regiment'.

His service record shows his children and their dates of birth to be:

George G * (sic) actually Geraldine	5 November 1883
George Vivian	6 December 1884
Griselda M (my grandmother)	7 November 1885
Jessie	6 December 1886
Lozzia E	9 February 1890
Victor J	7 February 1892
Emma	8 October 1893
Maud	31 August 1896

At first I thought nothing of the fact that Sergeant-Major Ash had named his first born son 'George'. I became puzzled when I couldn't find a reference to him in the births index. I was also puzzled at not being able to find my grandmother in the same births index (hoping to confirm the Tower of London point). What I was to prove later is that the reference to George G is an error presumably by the clerk taking down the details. Reference to a copy of her birth certificate which I obtained through the Family Records Centre in London, shows that Geraldine was born on 5 November 1883 AND that she was born in the Tower of London.

Anyway, what his service record shows is that he had eight children, two boys and six girls. I noted the production line of the first four years in particular and that the first born, Geraldine (not George) must have been a little premature! To discuss the girls, briefly, the intriguing thing about the list is that it introduces some new puzzles as well as confirming the memory of myself and my brother about our great aunts. Griselda, my grandmother is there and not being the old-est girl this does nothing to explain her family nickname 'Cissie'. Maud, the last born we remember too; but who are Jessie, Lozzia and Emma and where are

---

* After perplexing me and sending me down blind alleys, I worked out that this was a clerical error.

Sadie and Gertie? This could be explained by, say, infant or child deaths, by later births or great aunts being known by names other than their given names. What of the boys, Cissie's brothers, George Vivian and Victor John. Their names have no place in my memory nor that of my elder brother.

Throughout my life all references (such as they were) to Cissie's brothers were in relation to their being long deceased. I had it in mind that they may have all died in the Great War possibly at Gallipoli. Now that I had the names I could refer to the *Soldiers Died in the Great War* CD Rom. This shows neither George G nor Victor J, but it does show that Private 2007 George Vivian Ash of the 1st/5th Battalion, Lancashire Fusiliers was killed in action at Gallipoli on 4 June 1915. So there it was, George Vivian Ash, one of Cissie's brothers, did die at Gallipoli; my speculative remark to Len Chandler had been true. So at the end of my first visit to the Public Record Office my knowledge of Sergeant--Major Ash had moved up through a big step from the original gems supplied by the Lancashire Fusiliers Museum, moreover, it was only a few weeks since all that I knew was what it said on the inscription on the *'handsome timepiece'*. I had discovered that he had been a professional soldier for over 31 years - that he was a Dorset man (and not from Bury) and had served with the Scots Fusilier Guards, the Royal Fusiliers and the Lancashire Fusiliers - that he had served in Egypt and that one of his sons, my great uncle, had died at Gallipoli and was remembered at Helles, Turkey, and the names of his wife and family.

I was deeply impressed with how fast information could be found, at least if one is focused and determined. If I was well satisfied with my first day's trawl through hard copy, I was to be stunned by the discovery I made on the Internet that same evening. I wanted to find out something about the site where George Vivian was buried. I decided, somewhat speculatively, to go to the Commonwealth War Graves website on the Internet. I found that it was easy to enter the file listing the war dead and giving details of their graves. I decided to check each of the Sergeant-Major's sons' names. I found George Vivian and printed the notes on his grave reference and some historical information and his commemoration record. That I wasn't able to find George G was of course, because he didn't exist. I looked for Victor J but I couldn't find him either, unsurprisingly, because he was not on the *Soldiers Died in the Great War* CD Rom either. But can you imagine the shock when I found, when looking for George G, none other than George - yes, Sergeant-Major George Ash, my great grandfather, the very one who had retired on 31 March 1907 having spent then over 31 years in the Army.

So, father and son were both in the *Soldiers Died* file. The Commonwealth War Graves Commission file tells us that he died at home on 8th March 1915 at the age of 56! He is interred in Bury Cemetery (where evidently over 70 of his Great War comrades are also buried) and that he was the son of Robert and Jane Ash of Sydling St Nicholas in Dorset. Incontrovertible evidence had been found of where he started and where he had finished his days on earth, and I have his *handsome timepiece.*

To have gained all this knowledge from one day's work at Kew and on the Internet following the Lancashire Fusiliers input was deeply satisfying. I deserved my next visit to the Foley Arms to report into the chums. The link of Gallipoli between the ancestors of myself, Len Chandler and David Hare was now completed.

Although it was time to check in again with the Lancashire Fusiliers too with the new facts, the continuing muddle over who were the Sergeant-Major's children was something for me to research further. The 1891 census return would help but to access this at the Family Record Centre, Myddleton Street, London EC1, you need to know the residence address at the time of the census, it is the only way of accessing it. I decided to review what I knew about where the Sergeant-Major had been living.

I had established that he was born in Dorset in 1858 and enlisted there in 1875. I now knew from his service record that in 1882 he was in Egypt. He had married in 1883 (but I didn't know where), between 31 December 1886 and 21 March 1894 he was with the Royal Fusiliers (suggesting a London residence) and that from 1894 to 1907 he was in Bury with the Lancashire Fusiliers.

The *'Soldiers Died'* CD Rom had told me that Private George Vivian Ash had been born in Chelsea in 1884. Although I still didn't know where he was living at the time of the census I had gained a large quantity of hard evidence from primary sources. From the point of view of the need to locate the residential address in April 1891 the key was provided by the Sergeant-Major's will.

I had established the existence of a will at the PRO in Kew where the index told me that administration of the will had been granted to the Sergeant-Major's widow on 28th October 1915. My motive for going to the Probate Office in Holborn was to read the will to find if it gave any more clues about his family. What I found was that on 14 August 1890, George Ash (No. 1765 of the 4th Battalion, Royal Fusiliers, City of London Regiment) made a will leaving the whole of his estate to his wife Elizabeth, whose address was given as Finsbury Barracks, London EC. The executors were a couple of important sounding gentlemen from Mayfair and Chelsea. By a codicil dated 27 February 1905, he appointed his son George Vivian his sole executor, one of the previous appointees having died. The address of both father and son were at this time given as "Castle Armoury, Bury".

George Vivian was 20 years old at this time, so, either he was still living in the family home or he had himself joined up. * As will be recalled, the Sergeant-Major died on 8th March 1915 at 8, School Brow, Bury, and George Vivian on

---

* I discovered later that George Vivian Ash had been a member of the Lancashire Fusilier Territorials before the Great War.

4 June 1915. Evidently, George Vivian must have given his mother a Power of Attorney before he left for Egypt with the 1st/5th Battalion in September 1914 * because it was she who was granted Probate on 28 October 1915 when the gross value of his estate is noted as £370.

If the Sergeant-Major and his wife were living in Finsbury Barracks in August 1890 it required no great leap of mind to suppose that they might still be living there in April 1891. I had planned to visit the Probate Office and the Family Record Centre in the same day, the latter to investigate further dates and places of the Sergeant-Major's children (the Tower of London point), and his marriage. Equipped as I now was with a good hypothesis of where to look I could prioritise a search of the 1891 Census.

Although a first time visit to the census research facility is initially somewhat bewildering, there are archivists there who are most helpful. The records for 1891 are on large rolls of microfilm organised by street address in districts. The name of the district is not always obvious from the address but help is around to identify exactly where to look. Of course, all I knew of an address was "Finsbury Barracks", London EC. Happily, institutional census data in the nature of barracks were organised in the lists before the street addresses so it was easy to find.

I looked and there was the Ash family living in Finsbury Barracks on 5 April 1891. At that time none of either Victor J, Emma or Maud had been born but there were all the other children, Geraldine (not George G as noted earlier in this chapter), George Vivian, Griselda Myra (my grandmother), Jessie and Lozzia all with their ages noted and tallying exactly with the Sergeant-Major's service record in Kew allowing for the mistake of 'George' for 'Geraldine'! Also given were their places of birth, the Sergeant-Major, of course, in Sydling St Thomas, Dorset - Elizabeth Ash in Scotland (I had discovered that people moved around the country in Victorian times much more than might be assumed). Geraldine was shown as born in "Tower Liberty". I take this to mean the Tower while *at* liberty - that she was born in the Tower is confirmed by her birth certificate (subsequently obtained).

My grandmother is shown as being born in Ireland! Now, there was a surprise! This news, at least, explained why I could not find a record of my grandmother's birth in the England indexes. It also suggested that someone had been in a muddle about where they were born or (which I claim to be unlikely) my memory was at fault. I had, at least, remembered *a* connection with the Tower of London. Subsequently, I established from the Scots Guards that the 1st Battalion had been on garrison duty in Dublin for a year from September 1885 (my grandmother having been born in the November of that year). So there we have it.

Cissie was born in Dublin Castle and her elder sister was born in the Tower

---

* There was no thought of Gallipoli at this stage. They went to Egypt to form the garrison in order to release regular troops for France.

of London.   The other children alive at the time of the census, George Vivian, Jessie and Lozzia were all shown as having been born in Middlesex, London. Subsequently, I established from the Scots Guards that the 1st Battalion had been on garrison duty in Dublin for a year from September 1885. (my grandmother having been born in the November of that year).

Now that I knew that both the Sergeant-Major and George Vivian (at least) had served in the Great War, I returned quickly to Kew to try and find their Army service records, as I had done for the Sergeant-Major's earlier service.   This was to present me with my first setback.   Unhappily, about 60% of the records of soldiers who served in the Great War were destroyed in 1940 by enemy action.   Of those that survived, many are badly damaged by fire or water.   These records, I discovered, are referred to as *'The Burnt Records'*.   As I searched through the microfilm of The Burnt Records for all the Ash's of my family, I paused to reflect on the irony of the name, and their fate, for none of their records survived the fire in 1940 during the second war just as neither the Sergeant-Major nor George Vivian themselves had survived the first war.   On further enquiry I established that not only have some of these records been lost but there is no record of what was in the store that burned, therefore there is evidently no way of proving Army service in the Great War unless either the record has survived (only about 40%) or if the unfortunate man died.

Although this is surprising, i.e. that there was no separate list of the records that were in store, at least none that has been discovered, I am satisfied that the archivists at Kew are as frustrated as I was to be about this gap. I was left with the big open question of what became of Victor.

Notwithstanding this setback I had travelled an enormous distance in just three weeks.   Everything I have related so far, except where stated, was achieved in that period and it all started with a clock and the inscription on that clock.   On 28 March 2001 that was all I knew plus my memories of my grandmother and her bitter references to the Dardanelles, the Tower of London and my childhood visits to Bury.   There was a lot more to come.

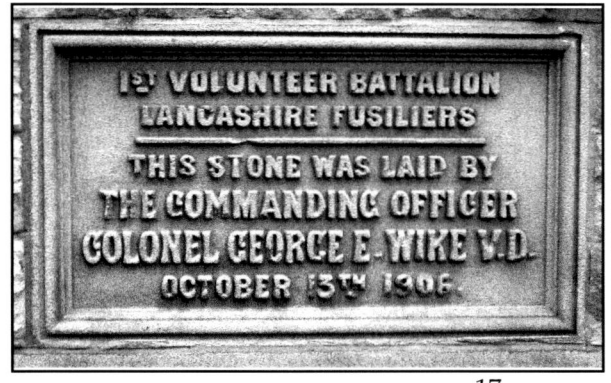

When Sgt-Major Ash rejoined the Army in 1914, he trained recruits at the Drill Hall at the Castle Armoury, Bury.   This photo (2003) shows that Colonel Wike laid the foundation stone in 1906, the year before he presented Sgt-Major Ash with the "handsome timepiece" on his retirement from the Army.   Colonel Wike was later wounded at Gallipoli.

(Author's photo 2003)

CHAPTER 3

Go and read the names

As the news of all the discoveries so far broke, my chums in the Foley Arms became more and more intrigued. That the Sergeant-Major had rejoined the Lancashire Fusiliers, after having previously served 31 years in the Army, and then his dying in service at the age of 56 , was quite a talking point because it was so surprising and unusual. I discovered later that the Army had included , in its quest for a volunteer army, a deliberate appeal to retired NCOs which it wanted to recruit so that it could mobilise the massive training effort demanded by the outbreak of war in August 1914. Sergeant-Major Ash had responded to the call to rejoin the regiment in spite of his age. This was not so uncommon, as I discovered.

The Commonwealth War Graves Commission head-stone at the grave of Sgt-Major Ash, Manchester Road Cemetery, Bury, where the firing party fired their volley.
(Author's photo, 2003)

Of course there was Private George Vivian Ash. I had discovered that he had served and died in Gallipoli with the 1st/5th Battalion of the Lancashire Fusiliers. They weren't supposed to be part of the Gallipoli campaign at all. They were ter-ritorials who had been in Egypt since September 1914 and their business was to be part of the garrison force that was holding the country, and later, after Turkey had entered the war on Germany's side, guarding the Suez Canal from attack.

It was an intriguing coincidence for both father and son to have served in a force mobilised for war in the same overseas station. It is easy to imagine the farewell from Bury when Sergeant-Major Ash would have been able to give his eldest son many tips about life in the desert and, more intriguingly, in Cairo. It is a some-what bizarre thought to imagine all these Lancashire lads from the mills, convers-ing in their own dialect, being let loose in Cairo when they had leave.

The name of Gallipoli - I knew nothing of it - was beginning to enter my being. An irresistible quest for knowledge of it rose within me. I had a sense of belonging, of communion even with all those for whom the name had some meaning greater than just a historical reference. I could feel within me, inexorably, a bonding with my grandmother as, over the next few weeks, my knowledge grew. As I have said, the Egyptian garrison should never have been involved in the Gallipoli campaign. If it had all gone according to its too optimistic but flawed plan, they wouldn't have been! It was only when things went wrong and the fighting was bogged down, that reinforcements were called in. I discovered that the Lancashire territorials had the misfortune to be in the wrong place at the wrong time. Many were to die and many more were to suffer. At this stage, all I knew was that Private George Vivian Ash had arrived on the peninsular in May and died soon after on 4 June 1915, and that like so many he has no known grave, but is 'Remembered with Honour' at the Helles Memorial on the Gallipoli peninsula in Turkey.

Having established all this there was now a real common connection between my great uncle Vivian, Len Chandler's father* and David Hare's grand-father. My man died at Gallipoli, both of their men had been wounded at Gallipoli but had survived. This engaging common interest was established and was to be a constant theme of conversation in the Foley Arms over the coming months.

Being a Brigadier-General, Hare's name was likely, I reasoned, to be referred to in the literature. I established that Brigadier-General Hare was in command of the 86th Brigade of which the 1st Battalion, the Lancashire Fusiliers (a regular battalion) was part. This is not to be confused with Private Ash's 1st/5th Battalion. In the chronology of my discoveries about the Lancashire Fusiliers, it was the exploits of the 1st Battalion at Gallipoli that I came across first.

---

* Private Frederick Chandler's story is one of those of the good news variety. A professional soldier in the 1st Battalion Border Regiment, he served successively from 1908 in India, the Andaman Islands (a penal settlement in the Bay of Bengal) and then Burma, until August 1914 when the Battalion returned to the UK to become part of the 87th Brigade, 29th Division. He landed at X beach at Gallipoli on 25 April 1915, survived the fighting at Helles during the summer, and was withdrawn for the new invasion at Suvla Bay in August. He was wounded in that fighting and was evacuated. He recovered in time to fight on the first day of the Battle of the Somme on 1st July 1916, where he was wounded. He recovered in time to be wounded twice more in France.

On being invalided out of the Army on 10th November 1918, he attended the Armistice Day celebrations next day dressed in civvies. *"Cor, you're lucky mate, its all over - you won't have to fight now"* came the friendly but unknowing comment from a stranger. He survived for 40 more years, dying in 1955.

On 25 April 1915, this regular battalion of Lancashire Fusiliers famously won "Six VCs before breakfast" on the first day of the landings at Cape Helles, Gallipoli.*

The Lancashire Fusiliers raised a total of thirty battalions in the Great War. Of all their deeds the transcending feat was the landing, on 25 April 1915, by the 1st Battalion on what was "W" beach but which was ordered to be renamed 'Lancashire Landing'. The battalion was carried close to the shore in HMS *Euryalus*. At 4:00 a.m. the companies transferred to small unpowered ships' boats, which were towed towards the shore by steam powered boats (pinnaces) from the warships. When about 50 yards from the shore the pinnaces cast off leaving the boats to be rowed to the beach by their naval crews, under covering fire from the warships. The Turks were waiting for them.

To realise the horror consider the following eye-witness account of Leading Seaman Gilligan from *Euryalus* in a letter to his vicar published in the *Bury Guardian* on 16 June 1915:-

*"We landed the Lancashire Fusiliers, 35 in each boat. I shall never forget it as long as I live. We lost 19-20 of our ship's company. I would not like to go through the same again. It was wicked and I, like a lot more, never expected to come through it whole. We landed at daybreak under a very heavy fire from our ship. It was deafening. There were four boats in tow of a steam pinnace, and there was no sign of the enemy till we touched the shore. Then they opened fire on us in the boats. They were very strongly entrenched above us in the cliffs, with Maxims, Nordenfeldts** and 1lb Pom Poms. I was in charge of No. 12 boat and I told the men to lie down in the bottom of the boat, leaving myself and six oarsmen exposed to the enemy's fire. I then ordered them all to jump out and get under cover as quickly as they could As soon as we touched the beach we could see wire entanglements. The fire was terrible, just like a hailstorm. I jumped out of the stern up to my arms in water and pushed the boat in. The Sergeant jumped in front of me and got mortally wounded. The cries of the wounded were terrible.*
By now the Lancashires were ashore. We came off for more men and one man was killed in my crew. I could mention a lot of cases, but they are better left for the present. I hope I am spared to tell you the thrilling story when I come home. It is without equal in this war, landing troops under fire. There is such a bond between the Lancashire Fusiliers and us now that it will never be broken by the -----*** that are left. I never thought I should come out clear, but we have done well."

Indeed they had. As we shall soon see, Leading Seaman Gilligan was spot on when he predicted that the bond between the 1st Battalion and the ship's company of *Euryalus* would never be broken.

---

*Before the Lancashire Landing, the most celebrated feat of the XXth Regiment of Foot (the earlier name of the Lancashire Fusiliers) had been the battle of Minden on 1st August 1759. It is still celebrated today as *Minden Day*.

** Automatic weapons.

*** Here the dead hand of the censor obliterates the number of survivors.

The commander in chief, General Sir Ian Hamilton had a good view of the landing. He wrote in his dispatch:-

".....So strong, in fact, were the defences of W beach that the Turks may well have considered them impregnable, and it is my firm conviction that no finer feat of arms has ever been achieved by the British soldier - or any other soldier - than the storming of these beaches from open boats on the morning of 25th April.
The landing at W had been entrusted to the 1st Battalion Lancashire Fusiliers (Major Bishop) and it was to the complete lack of the senses of danger or of fear of this daring battalion that we owed our astonishing success....
Gallantly led by their officers, the Fusiliers literally hurled themselves ashore and fired at from right, left and centre, commenced hacking their way through the wire. A long line of men was at once mown down as by a scythe, but the remainder were not to be denied...."

Vice-Admiral De Roebeck the commander of the Naval Force, in his dispatch on the naval aspect of the operation, wrote:-

"....It is impossible to exalt too highly the service rendered by the 1st Battalion Lancashire Fusiliers in the storming of the beach; the dash and gallantry displayed was superb...."

From *Euryalus* herself came another intimate tribute:-

"We are as proud as can be to have had the honour to carry your splendid regiment. We feel for you all in your great losses as if you were our own ship's company, but know the magnificent gallantry of your regiment has made the name more famous than ever."

The Royal Navy itself had had 63 out of 80 ratings killed or wounded in the operation that became known as *'Lancashire Landing'*.*
    These words of praise, given as they were independently of each other, offer an exalted testimony. From that moment there was created an unbreakable bond between the ship's company of HMS *Euryalus* and the Lancashire Fusiliers which survives today through the Euryalus Veterans' Association. In a magnificent gesture, the ship's company erected a fine tablet to the memory of the *Lancashire Landing* in Bury Parish Church. It was unveiled in 1930 by Admiral of the Fleet, Lord Wemyss (who had flown his flag in *Euryalus* at the time). The inscription reads:

'LANCASHIRE LANDING'
TO COMMEMORATE
THE OFFICERS
NON-COMMISSIONED OFFICERS

---

* *Regiment of the Line*: Cyril Ray, 1963.

AND MEN OF
THE FIRST BATTALION
THE LANCASHIRE FUSILIERS
WHO FELL IN ACTION
AT GALLIPOLI IN 1915
THIS TABLET
IS PLACED HERE BY THE
OFFICERS AND SHIP'S COMPANY OF
H.M.S. EURYALUS
THE SHIP WHICH LANDED THE
FUSILIERS AT CAPE HELLES
APRIL 25TH, 1915

The ship's battle flag that was flown at the time of the landing was also lodged in Bury Parish Church.

A silver model of a cutter from HMS *Euryalus*, photographed by the author in the officer's mess, 2nd Battalion Royal Regiment of Fusiliers, North Luffenham, 2003

Euryalus, a Crecy Class cruiser, whose name is indissolubly linked to the Lancashire Fusiliers by a bond that was forged on 25 April 1915.
(Courtesy Imperial War Museum, negative number Q38828)

That the bond between Euryalus and the 1st Battalion is lock tight is proved by the fact that the several successor warships bearing the same name have continued to celebrate the link. I was deeply impressed to learn that when the vessel was decommissioned in 1934 her watch bell - the one that had counted the hours at Cape Helles - was donated by the Admiralty to 1st Battalion, Lancashire Fusiliers. It remains still with 1st Battalion, Royal Regiment of Fusiliers, the successor regiment, and it goes with them wherever they go. Presently it is in Germany.

During the Second World War, the 5th *Euryalus* was a *Dido* class cruiser. When she was placed in reserve in 1954, her ship's crest was also presented to the 1st Battalion and her bell to the Recruit Training Regiment at Bassingbourn, near Cambridge. The 6th and last HMS Euryalus, a frigate was decommissioned in 1989. Her ship's bell is in the Lancashire Fusiliers Museum in Bury, as is her deck plate name.

Shortly after I had first discovered this kinship between serving and former members of the ships' companies of *Euryalus* and the Lancashire Fusiliers, I was able to receive graphic illustration of the intensity of it. I had a chance conversation with a fellow guest at a wedding reception. It turned out that he had served with the Lancashire Fusiliers as a junior officer in the 1950s. I asked him about HMS *Euryalus.* He told me a story to reinforce the tradition. Evidently, my story relater was stationed with his battalion in Aqaba* when, providentially, the then *Euryalus* - this would be the *Dido* class cruiser - called at the port.

My 2nd Lieutenant raconteur told me, the celebrations having got a bit out of hand, that he had been placed under *'tent arrest'* having been fished out of Aqaba harbour *"wearing a Matelot's cap".* Evidently fortune was with this young man, whose behaviour was no doubt regarded as quite improper for an officer, because, with *Euryalus* involved, the circumstances were thought to be extenuating. The reader should be reminded that this story is from the 1950s, some forty years since a predecessor vessel had carried the 1st Battalion to immortality on 25 April 1915 - Gallipoli Day.

As the *Bury Times* tells its readers in the modern age 85 years later, Gallipoli Day, April 25, is an honoured anniversary in the Regiment. 'In Memoriam' notices are inserted in London and Lancashire newspapers for all ranks of the 1st Battalion who died at the Lancashire Landing. 'Gallipoli greetings' are exchanged between units, and are sent from the Colonel of the Regiment to all units, to HMS *Euryalus* when in commission and to senior officers of the Regiment.

---

*   Aqaba is a port at the head of the Gulf of Aqaba at the head of the Red Sea. Famously, Lawrence of Arabia captured it from the Turks in 1917 with a handful of men attacking from inland having crossed the desert in an epic journey celebrated in the film *Lawrence of Arabia.* Infamously, the Turks' guns were pointing out to sea from where an attack was feared and they were defenceless from the rear.
Twenty six years later, Singapore was to fall to the Japanese, cheaply and disgracefully, for the same reason. Plus ca change!

Also included when they were still surviving, were the regimental holders of the Victoria Cross. The 1st Battalion parades, and maintains a two minute silence followed by the 'Last Post' sounded, when possible, on the silver bugle presented by the fifth Euryalus to commemorate the service together of the ship and the 11th Battalion during the siege of Malta in 1942. Afterwards all ranks are given an opportunity to see the Colours, the Regimental Rolls of Honour and trophies.

On the Sunday closest to April 25, a Commemoration Service is held in Bury Parish Church, attended by the Mayor and Corporation and civic dignitaries of the town, detachments of the Regiment, Old Comrades' Associations, the Royal British Legion, ex members and friends of the Regiment. Wreaths are laid on the Regimental Memorial at Wellington Barracks, the Euryalus memorial tablet in the Church, and the Bury War Memorial. After the service there is a march past and the Colonel of the Regiment and the Mayor take the salute. It is now regarded as the annual commemoration of all the Regiment's dead. Thus is the culture of Bury entwined with the Lancashire Fusiliers, and through them, Gallipoli.

Before long Len Chandler introduced both myself and David Hare to The Gallipoli Association, whose objective is to preserve the memory of the men who served in and to commemorate the events of The Dardanelles campaign from April 1915 to January 1916. Although it is not very old - it was founded in 1969 - it is growing and has over 1,000 members who are authors, amateur historians, or those who have a special interest in remembering, often because of a family connection. As one of those it was natural for David Hare and I to join as had Len Chandler before us. Its genesis may explain why it thrives today. Most similar organisations grew out of veterans' associations, which, by their nature have difficulty surviving the lives of their members. There was never a veterans' association for Gallipoli, and neither was there a campaign medal.

The Gallipoli Association seems to thrive because of a continuing, and to some extent rekindled public interest in an evocative campaign from a historical point of view, possibly because the Great War is studied at school now, whereas it wasn't until about 20 or 30 years ago, but also from second and now third generation descendants of the hundreds of thousands of the Allied participants in the campaign. Equally, the campaign has huge numbers of lessons for the military student and not just in the obvious field of amphibious warfare, although the lessons in this respect are signal. The lessons go to the heart of political and military control of warfare, and, assuming these to be in harmony, the unified command structure required for effective control over all the resources available to a mission. The lessons of communications, intelligence and the need to move inland quickly to gain the heights are vividly illustrated by the errors of the campaign.

In one respect the campaign had a remarkable success and that was that, once the political decision was made to evacuate, a new man replaced the

Commander-in Chief,* and he pulled off such a remarkable stroke of tactical deception and logistical execution that he was able to re-embark the whole force on the peninsular without loss.   This is a reason to celebrate the ending of the campaign (from a purely military view) but on its own goes nowhere near explaining the popular interest in it.   It has been said that it is a characteristic of the British people to be disposed to see in these skillful evacuations, under the enemy's nose, and without loss, some sort of 'victory'.   There are those who will always be pleased with successful military operations, even if they are going backwards.   Dunkirk in 1940 was an astonishing retreat, rearguard action and evacuation, which Churchill was careful to characterise as a *deliverance* - *"Wars are not won by evacuations"* he was to warn when the British people saw in it a victory.   Victory it was not, but to achieve the means of survival, which it certainly was, is to mark a fulcrum point in history which will be celebrated forever.

So it was for the Turks.   Their victory at Gallipoli was their survival.   It took the defeat of Germany on the Western Front three terrible years later to take it from them, but the truth is that the British and French failure at Gallipoli was one of the worst disasters in British history.   As it turned out, the campaign had no effect on the war and I was to discover that there were some good judges who doubted that it ever could.

I knew none of this, for I was only just beginning to have any knowledge where Gallipoli was concerned, but I could feel myself being drawn towards it both physically and in an inexorable quest for knowledge and understanding of the momentous events.   As I began to discover the awful cost to the men of Bury and Lancashire through the scale of the carnage, I could feel myself too being drawn back to that town of childhood memories.   It makes me weep now to recall my grandmother holding back tears as she spat the name 'The Dardanelles'. How ignorant I was.   I didn't know her brother had died.   She never said, she only alluded.   I didn't know about the suffering of the Lancashire Fusiliers.   I didn't know about Gallipoli Sunday.   I was never told any of these things.   Why not?   I could only feel that there was something tragic that connected the Lancashire Fusiliers and the Dardanelles campaign.

That I didn't know, that I hadn't been told, was the beginning of a slowly growing but containable anger that started without me even knowing.   It was latent within me at first but later, after some tears and some more discoveries - some profound, some quite impossible to predict or to create in a dream of fantasies - I was to discover that the story brought out the same emotion in my brother, a man who, while not so interested as me in history and war, has had the same cultural inputs into his upbringing as I had.   He felt a mild anger too at not

---

* This was Lieutenant-General Sir C Monro. There is an interesting parallel here with the practice of management in business. In project management it has been observed that managers with different skills are valuable in different phases of the life cycle of a project; at the tail of a project, for example, particular skills analogous to those of a good commander of a military withdrawal are appropriate.

being told of some of the things I was to discover; a definite emotion born out of an expectation that there are some things that should not be choked out of family culture. Honourable things should be honoured - and remembered.

Just in case my grandmother (to whom this criticism must chiefly be aimed, along with my Great Aunties - Sadie and Maud- who both inhabited my childhood - my mother was not yet four when George Vivian died in Gallipoli) - just in case they can observe me penning this criticism, I have developed a hypothesis of how it might have happened. The reader will recall that I have said there were never any men in my mother's family.

We have seen that Sergeant-Major Ash and his son George Vivian died in the Great War. Even after all my research I still have no knowledge of the fate of Victor J but I can say that I had never heard my mother speak of him so it is doubtful if he ever entered her consciousness. So, my mother grew up with no brothers, a father who didn't serve in the Great War because he was unfit and no uncles. Everyone has their own coping strategy for life after a trauma, perhaps the coping strategy for Cissie and her sisters was to close down the subject. Anyway, close down they all did; on the Dardanelles, except in anger and as a rebuke; on the deaths in the family, except obliquely and on much, much more as I was to discover, but they didn't hold back on 'the esteem in which Sergeant-Major Ash was held. This part of the family culture was handed down in permanent ink. It was deeply inbred and as I was to discover, by not one jot or tittle was it exaggerated.

For the moment, however, it was to Bury that I was drawn and to the Lancashire Fusiliers. I had a need to visit the Sergeant-Major's grave in the cemetery in Bury. It was a call that many a descendant of the military fallen have heard - a compulsive need to experience the catharsis of how or where the end came. I wanted to go and read the names in Bury.

I resolved to plan a week in Bury for this purpose and to pursue a few research sources in the town. Just as the trip was being planned, the Spring edition of The Gallipolian (the journal of the Gallipoli Association) arrived. The following poem appeared. I am greatly indebted to Ian Davidson and Friends of the Laurel for kind permission to reproduce this poem by Ken Stephens.

GO AND READ THE NAMES

CHORUS
Go and read the names, go and read the names,
In city or in hamlets the list is just the same,
Peace forever more they said, never mind the blame,
Don't let it all begin again, just go and read the names.
****

In market square or village green or country churchyard old,
You will find a list inscribed as the Honour Roll,
Cast away in youth and prime to die by bombs or flames,
And if you don't believe it, go and read the names.
****

`O'er land and sea men went to fight forsaking daily chores,
Each within their hearts thought it would quickly end all wars.
Some paid the greatest sacrifice and needlessly were slain,
And if you don't believe it, go and read the names.
****

Highborn Lord and Country Squire, clerk and factory hand,
The flower of generations all across the land.
The cause was right, the call was made, and willingly they came,
And if you don't believe it, go and read the names.
****

The tablets may have verdigris and the stonework flakes away,
But the terrible message of the past is close to us today.
So purge the anger from your hearts, don't condemn us to the flames
And don't think it can't happen, go and read the names.
****

I was surprised to find that the War Memorial outside Bury Parish Church carries no names of the dead. This assuaged my anger a little because I was no longer able to question why I, as a child, had not been taken by my grandmother to "go and read the names". That there are no names on the memorial saddened me. I was left conjecturing that there were too many names to fit on a memorial. The Lancashire Fusiliers maintain a Roll of Honour of the fallen in the Great War; it contains the names of 13,642 officers and men. Later in my research I established the reality of the scale of Bury's own losses of men. To have inscribed the names on a memorial would have required a minor version of the Wall of Remembrance to the fallen of the Vietnam War in Washington DC. There is a memorial in the Drill Hall, Bury, to all those members of the Bury Territorials (i.e. local men) who fell in the Great War. The memorial refers to the principal battles fought by the Bury Territorial Battalions (i.e. the 5th) at Helles, Rumani, Ypres and Bapaume. It reads:-

**IN PROUD MEMORY
OF 1662 OFFICERS AND MEN
OF THE 1st/5th/2nd/5th AND 3rd/5th BATTALIONS
THE LANCASHIRE FUSILIERS
WHO LAID DOWN THEIR LIVES
FOR THEIR COUNTRY**

Can you imagine? A town of 50,000 or so population which loses 1662 of its men. This is the scale of the suffering of Bury. Add in the families touched by the battle casualties who survived and you begin to understand the degree of the human impact of such a tragedy. Perhaps, I was thinking, this does explain why I wasn't told. Perhaps it was just too much to bear for my grandmother and her family, so they closed down on the subject. A clergyman in Bury told me that it was a common coping strategy even if it were intuitive rather than conspiratorial.

I was to discover later that the name of Private George Vivian Ash was remembered on the Roll of Honour of Bury Church School. I went to the successor school only to discover that the honour board was not displayed there. Evidently, the old school building has been demolished and no-one knows where the honour board is. Saddened, I had to give up on this one hoping one day to read the name at Helles.

Anyway, I still had to find the grave of Sergeant-Major Ash. I found the cemetery easily enough at Redvales, Bury, off Manchester Road only some three-quarters of a mile from where my grandparents had lived. In the words of my brother, when I told him I had found the grave of Sergeant-Major Ash and where it was:- "But we've been past the end of that road 50 times!" We had, but we had never been taken to see the grave nor been told it was there. We will never know why not. I have serious doubts about whether my mother was ever taken. She was four years old when the Sergeant-Major died. I am certain she would have made references to the grave if she had known it was there.

According to the Commonwealth War Graves Commission register of war dead on HYPERLINK "http://www.cwgc.org" there are over 70 graves from the Great War and nearly 60 from the Second World War in Bury Cemetery. I have seen the work of the Commonwealth War Graves Commission in Flanders, Normandy, Germany, Salerno, Cassino and El Alamein - all glorious monuments to the dead to whom our freedom is owed. Glorious in their design, their setting and the painstaking care with which they are maintained. My expectations as I approached the Manchester Road Cemetery in Bury were pitched at far too high a level *"Where are the war graves?"* I cheerfully asked a groundsman, only to be deflated by his reply:- *"How long have you got?"* I had expected that there would be *"...some corner of a ... field that was forever England"* to quote scantily Rupert Brooke.* In fact all the Commonwealth War Graves Commission graves in Bury Cemetery are randomly distributed through a very large but pleasantly wooded scene, the dead being buried on plots where they were available at the time of the soldiers' deaths, usually, one assumes, from wounds or disease.

---

* Rupert Brooke, the celebrated and much mourned war poet, died on 23 April 1915 of blood poisoning, on his way to serve at Gallipoli with the Hood Battalion, the Royal Naval Division.

Knowing the plot number from the HYPERLINK I was able to find the grave without much difficulty. The headstone was the familiar Portland stone engraved in the usual way. The dedication, which as I understand it is given to the next of kin to choose, is :- *"Peace, perfect peace"*. It comes from *"Songs in the House of Pilgrimage"* (1875 by E.H. Bickersteth, an English clergyman who died in 1906). It is all too easy to imagine that Elizabeth Ash was not to enjoy the peace she wished the Sergeant-Major for some time. Her troubles were only just beginning.

It frightens me to remember, when at the grave, how close I came to failing to observe the poppy. There was a poppy on the grave which I didn't see until I looked for a second time. It was large, secured to the ground by a long wire and faded by the light. How long it had been there I couldn't be sure. It was June. Possibly since the previous November but conceivably longer judging by the extreme fading of the green of the leaf which had become a light buff in colour.

I looked around to see if any of the other Commonwealth War Graves were honoured with a poppy, but none was. Why, I wondered, would a grave of 85 years be honoured except by someone with a special reason? It couldn't be a contemporary - it was unlikely to be the descendant of a contemporary, the interest would be too remote. My hypothesis is that there is some descendant of the Sergeant-Major out there who still honours him.

It was only a simple step of thought to decide to leave a 'calling card' on the grave to see what would emerge. Later in the summer I returned to Bury to leave the following message on the grave:-

ANYONE INTERESTED
IN
SERGEANT-MAJOR ASH?

If you have any information on Sergeant-Major George Ash please get in touch with his great-grandson at the above address: he would very much like to hear from anyone with a connection with George Ash and his family.

Chapter 4

The Sergeant-Major's Funeral

As I drove to Bury early that June Monday morning I was in two minds with my emotions. I had no doubt that I would 'read the names', nor that I could enjoy the Lancashire Fusiliers' Museum but I did wonder, silently, whether I might come back empty handed so far as primary evidence on Sergeant-Major Ash or Private George Vivian Ash were concerned. I need not have been concerned; as I drove home the following Thursday I had within me a stock of exaltations of which dreams could not have been dreamed.

I spent the first day in Bury getting used to the town again. Much of it was unrecognisable - some few parts were instantly familiar. I went to the cemetery and the war memorial as already related. I re-visited Grosvenor Street, which was substantially unchanged. There are cars parked in the street now and everything seems to be in colour - my memory of it and other places in Bury was in monochrome. I went to the goods yard (the one where night shunting kept me awake and during which the Sergeant-Major's clock chimes gave me comfort) and gazed again into the void over the bridge on Market Street. On account of the decline that had taken place in the railways since my last visit to Bury in about the mid 1950s I was not at all surprised, but just a little disappointed, that there was no discernable evidence remaining of that vast space where shunting locos had toiled all night.

I had booked time with the reference library to search the microfilm archive of the *Bury Times.* Even as a child I had warm feelings towards the newspaper. It was not that I was a precocious reader or anything of that nature, it was simply that the *Bury Times* was regarded in such elevated terms by my mother that in the 1940s and 1950s my grandmother would post each twice-weekly edition, once read and digested, to my mother some 60 miles away in York so she could keep up with the Bury news. How she looked forward to it coming. I looked forward equally, simply because sometimes within the folds of the *Bury Times* would come a couple of sweets, rationed in those days, but nonetheless a regular source of expectation and joy. The sweets, if they came, had to be shared with my brother, but it was I who had the pleasure and excitement of waiting for the postman to call for I was too young then to have been packed off to school with my bread and dripping snack.

I thought I might find some little snippet announcing the Sergeant-Major's death - I dared have no greater expectation! Anyone who has tried to operate a microfilm reader will know how awkward they are until a certain dexterity is learned. I knew I wanted to start scanning in the first edition after the Sergeant-Major had died. After many wild gyrations with the film going too far this way then too far that, I finally managed to fix in the frame the front page of the edition of Wednesday 10 March 1915 (he having died on Monday 8 March). The first thing I noticed was the logo of the *Bury Times*. It looked just the same as I remembered it when it arrived in York as a wrapper for my sweets. Having taken in the deep draught of nostalgia with the recognition of the logo, I settled myself to begin what I thought might be the tedious process of visually scanning through the paper page by page.

As I settled into my chair to begin the process an image struck me - a photograph of a military gentleman - and then my eyes darted quickly to the headline:-

---

"DEATH OF SERGEANT-MAJOR ASH"

———

"HONOURABLE MILITARY CAREER"

———

I let out an audible sigh. Relief was quickly overtaken by new emotions. The headline covered a 750 word story and obituary of Sergeant-Major Ash, which I read quickly in amazement and awe. The report commenced:-

"We regret to announce the death of Sergeant-Major George Ash, which took place with rather painful suddenness at his residence, 8, School Brow, Bury, shortly after one o'clock on Monday morning. He was 56 years of age, and had been suffering from heart weakness for some time, but had been able to attend to his duties in connection with the Lancashire Fusiliers Territorials. Last week he obtained leave of absence from Friday until Monday and went to Blackpool, returning on Sunday night, and later was taken suddenly ill and expired from heart failure."
"A native of Dorchester, he enlisted in the 1st Scots Guards, and rose to the rank of Colour-Sergeant. He also served in the Coldstream Guards **[this is an error]** and took part in the Egyptian War in 1882, and was awarded the Egyptian war medal and the Khedive's bronze star. He was in the Guards about twenty years **[11 years in fact]** and afterwards was for two or three years **[8 years in fact]** a Colour-Sergeant in the Royal Fusiliers Militia. On the 21st March 1894, he came to Bury as Sergeant-Major of the 1st Volunteer Battalion Lancashire Fusiliers, and he served in that capacity for thirteen years, retiring in March 1907, his last parade with the battalion being on March 2nd in that year."

There is no evidence in Sergeant-Major Ash's service record at Kew to support the reference to the Coldstream Guards. His record shows that he transferred from the Scots Guards to the 4th Battalion, Royal Fusiliers on 31 December 1886 and served with them for eight years before joining the Lancashire Fusiliers.

Later research was to reveal another local paper, the *Bury Guardian*, of which I had been unaware, which carried its own report of the Sergeant Major's death.

The *Guardian* report said that:-

"He joined the Army as a youth and was on active service with the Guards in Egypt under.... Sir Garnet Wolseley. It was when Arabi Pasha threatened the Suez Canal that the British troops went to Egypt. He was with the Brigade of Guards which had many trying marches in a tropical climate of Alexandria when they embarked for Ismailia, where they were for two days. Forced marches followed and they were carried out under the immediate command of HRH The Duke of Connaught. They met the enemy, and after a short but sharp resistance they retired but not without succeeding in damming ... [the Sweetwater] Canal. The Guards were employed several days removing the dam, working up to their necks in water. Sudden orders saw them again on the move, and the work terminated on 19 September 1882 with the Battle of Tel El-Kebir in which Sergeant-Major Ash took part. They then proceeded to Cairo where they occupied the Citadel."

This was amazingly detailed. I knew from his service record at Kew that he had served in the Egyptian campaign but to have this detail brought it all alive and made me want to know more. The *Bury Times* reporter must have been quick off the blocks too after the Sergeant-Major's death because his report continues with fresh material which must have been gained from an interview with an officer in Bury, for it continues:-

"Sergeant-Major Ash was an energetic and painstaking officer, and kind and courteous to those with whom he had to deal, and he was held in high esteem by both officers and men. In camp he was indispensable, and the hills of North Wales, in the district where the Volunteers had their annual training,* were quite familiar to him, and he could easily find his way about."

We have already seen that the Sergeant-Major was held in high esteem by his family. Now we have evidence that it was general among his regimental colleagues!

The source of the next part of the report is not at all easy to fathom. The source could not possibly be Colonel Wike himself because I have established that at that time he was in Gallipoli. He was wounded two months later in the retreat from the Third Battle of Krithia in which battle Private George Vivian Ash died. Whoever the source was, he knew what was said on Sergeant Major Ash's retirement in 1907 because the report continues:-

"On his retirement from the Volunteers Colonel George E.Wike, the then commanding officer, paid a high tribute to his character and conduct. He pointed out that in addition to the Egyptian war medal and bronze star given by the Khedive, Sergeant-Major Ash possessed the long service and good conduct medal, which could only be gained by

---

* This was at Conway. I have seen photos of these camps taken from the air. The bell tents to sleep perhaps 4,000 men were pitched in blocks, which, like ranks of dressed soldiers, seemed to have been pitched in inch perfect order.

> twenty years exceedingly good conduct. [and] ... there had to be long service and irreproachable character and conduct, and that the Sergeant-Major had preserved for twenty years."

The language is somewhat dated now, but evidently Colonel Wike:-

> "...was one of a small committee who selected Sergeant-Major Ash, and they had never regretted the step they took, as he had carried out that "irreproachable character and conduct" he gained during the whole thirteen years he had been with them. The Guards had a good reputation for smartness and efficiency generally, and Sergeant-Major Ash had certainly held that up to them."

The *Bury Times* reported that Sergeant-Major Ash said that when he joined the Army he did so with the determination that he would serve Her Majesty the Queen faithfully, and he had followed out that determination; it was a joy and gladness to him to feel that he had done so. It is interesting to speculate how this sentiment came to be reported - it didn't come from the grave! I wonder if Colour-Sergeant Hickie was involved because evidence was mounting that they were very close.

The report continues:- *"On retiring from the Volunteer Force Sergeant-Major Ash became licensee of the Grey Mare Hotel, Bury."* This I had already discovered from his discharge papers at Kew but it was news to read that subsequently he had become the licensee of the Nob Inn, Little Lever, a canal-side pub about five miles away between Bury and Bolton on the Manchester, Bury and Bolton Canal which closed to navigation in 1961. The pub appears not to have survived the canal's closure for very long, but it survives still as a private house.

Now the report told me for the first time, the circumstances in which after the outbreak of the war George Ash had rejoined the Lancashire Fusiliers on October 4th, *"and again occupied the orderly room at the Bury Drill Hall...."* We are told that consistently with before he retired, his work was characterised by his energy. He gave up the tenancy of the Nob Inn, Little Lever, in January 1915, presumably because it was incompatible with his regimental duties, and subsequently *"came to reside at School Brow, Bury".*

The report tells us that Sergeant-Major Ash left a widow, two sons and five daughters. I had already established that at the time of the 1891 census he had six daughters. By a process of elimination I established that Emma must have died. This will explain why neither my brother nor me had heard of her. Having established that Geraldine (the eldest child) was alive at this time, the mystery remains how "Cissie' (my grandmother) acquired her nickname. It also leaves the mystery of how she came to inherit the *'handsome timepiece"* from her mother. What became of the Sergeant-Major's medals remains a mystery too.

Thanks to the *Bury Times* coverage of the Sergeant-Major's death and funeral, I was able to learn substantive facts about the Ash family - who had married whom including, most importantly, the new married names of the daughters, and to learn about his four grandchildren. This was my first new input of family information since a few weeks earlier when I had looked at the 1891 census which gave me information which had become 24 years out of date. This was specially true of Private George Vivian Ash, the Sergeant-Major's eldest son of whom all I knew at this time was his date and place of birth and death. The *Bury Times* tells us that he had served in the local Volunteer Force and was a bugler for some time; that he was chief clerk in the Bury Corporation Tramway office, and that presently he was with the 5th Territorial Battalion in Egypt.

I subsequently established that as Territorials they were not obliged to serve overseas but were available for home defence only. Almost to a man they all volunteered to serve anywhere and it was to Egypt they went, on garrison duty at first, but ultimately to suffering and inglorious defeat at Gallipoli.

The report confirmed that the funeral would be of a military character and that the Rector of Bury, the Rev. J.C. Hill* would conduct the service at Bury Parish Church.

In the next edition of the *Bury Times* was reported the following:-

---

"BRIGADE COMMANDER'S APPRECIATION."

"The Brigade Commander has learned with regret of the sudden death of Sergeant-Major Ash, of the depot 2nd/5th Battalion Lancashire Fusiliers at Bury. His example and soldierly spirit were most helpful to the young soldiers there and he will be much missed."

This small item brought to public attention that the appreciation of Sergeant-Major Ash was being expressed at a very high level in the regiment. I could scarcely wait, of course, to position the next edition of the *Bury Times* in the microfilm reader. This time there was a 700 word report on the funeral on the back page under the headline:-

---

THE LATE SERGEANT-MAJOR ASH.
"MILITARY FUNERAL."

"The remains of the late Sergeant-Major George Ash... were interred at the Bury Cemetery on Thursday afternoon. The deceased had served 35 years in the Army and Auxiliary Forces, and the funeral was of a military character and was witnessed by thousands of spectators."

I was to establish later the evidence to support the reference to "thousands" attending the Sergeant-Major's funeral. The cortege consisted of a firing party, the depot band, a hearse, three coaches and a brougham containing floral tributes. Many of the Territorial soldiers were evidently in civilian clothes.

---

* As we shall see later, Rev.Hill was to suffer his own tragic bereavement.

Perhaps they had been released from their day jobs, but according to the *Bury Times* *"were well dressed and respectable looking, showing the good class of men from which the battalion is recruited"*. The press in those days was content to adulate army service as a strong and laudable cultural thread of the town's life.

On the way from School Brow to the church the band played Chopin's Funeral March, which, the reporter said, was very impressive. The report was extraordinary in its detail giving a long list of many of the officers and NCO's of the regiment. The list included Colour-Sergeant Hickie. This was the man who retired on the same day as George Ash - he had rejoined the Army too! I read with some emotion that "the coffin... was covered with a Union Jack and had upon it the deceased's busby, sword and belt and a floral tribute."

The band of the Lancashire Fusiliers Territorials arrives at Bury Parish Church leading the funeral party for Sergeant-Major Ash. 11 March 1815.
(Courtesy, North West Film Archive at Manchester Metropolitan University)

The firing party of Territorial soldiers of the Lancashire Fusiliers process to the church with 'Arms in reverse'.
(Courtesy: North West Film Archive at Manchester Metropolitan University).

Part of the 'crowd of thousands' as reported by the *Bury Times,* who attended Sergeant-Major Ash's funeral.
(Courtesy, North West Film Archive at Manchester Metropolitan University)

The hearse carrying Sergeant-Major Ash's coffin arrives outside Bury Parish Church. The honour guard has already taken up position.
(Courtesy, North West Film Archive at Manchester Metropolitan University)

The coffin of Sergeant-Major Ash, his busby on top, is borne up the steps of Bury Parish Church, past the honour guard.
(Courtesy, North West Film Archive at Manchester Metropolitan University)

The report was far too long to hold the interests of my readers, but it contained definitive references to family members enabling me, by later research, to get a fix on who was married to whom. *"The principal mourners were:- In the first carriage - Mrs. Ash (widow), Mr. Victor Ash (son),* [seemingly not married and not in the army] *Misses Lizzie, Gertrude and Maud Ash (daughters)* [these three were obviously not yet married] *and Mrs. G.V. Ash (daughter-in-law)"* - this would have been Bessie Rawson who married George Vivian Ash on 29 January 1913 in Bury. At the time of the funeral he was, of course, in Egypt.

The next part of the report brought a lump to my throat:- *"In the second carriage were Mr. and Mrs. H. Barlow (son-in-law and daughter)* [these were my grandparents, Harry and Cissie Barlow, who were married on 8 August, 1908 in Bury] *and Mr. G.W. Day (son-in-law)"* This was very strange. Where was Mrs. Day, who as Jessie Ash had married George William Day on 13 December 1905 in Bury. I can only suppose that she was ill that day for she and her husband's name appeared together on a floral tribute. Also in the second carriage was *"Miss Emma Ash"*, youngest sister of the Sergeant-Major, and of whom I can write this vignette.

I have discovered no evidence of Emma Ash having married, for at the time of the funeral she was a 44 year old spinster. She had been only four years old when George Ash left Sydling to join the Scots Guards in 1875. The last trace I have of her was in Sydling, living with her mother and in domestic service. I do not know exactly where she was living at the time of the funeral but I think it almost certain she was still near her family home in Dorset.

If she was living in Dorset, imagine the logistics of how she got to the funeral. Her brother died early on the Monday and the funeral was on Wednesday. In the days before the telephone is likely to connect a poor spinster in domestic service in rural Dorset she must have received the news by telegram. I can imagine some Flora Thompson* type of character going about her Post Office chores when the bell sounded to signal an incoming telegram. How many of those would she have to deal with in a working day in a Dorset village? Not many yet I surmise, but later in the war there would be too many, mostly bearing grief for a mother and her family. And so it was with this one for Emma. Our Flora Thompson would read it as it ticked through her telegraph machine. She would know Emma well if not intimately, to whom it was addressed and summon a messenger boy to deliver the grim message telling her of her brother's death.

If this surmise is correct, Emma must have packed her bags more or less straight away and made the arrangements to make the 115 mile rail journey to London and then the 200 mile journey to Manchester and then on a local train to Bury. What a remarkable adventure. How amazed she must have been to observe, almost certainly for the first time in her life, an industrial region let alone a grimy smoke-stacked town like Bury and to have witnessed a crowd of thousands who attended her brother's funeral.

It must have been an as uplifting happening as she had ever experienced, one from another world which she dipped into for a day, and then returned to her simple country life. When she returned to Dorset she would have memories of the large crowd of spectators at the graveside with police preventing them encroaching too close, of the three volleys fired over the grave, and the bugler sounding the "Last Post", and as the *Bury Times* also reported, the band returning from the cemetery playing lively marches.

I have already referred to the extraordinary detail of the *Bury Times* report. It would tax my readers too much to detail the lengthy report of the floral tributes to the Sergeant-Major. I will risk just a brief account! One of the floral tributes came from *"Cissie, Harry and Baby"*. "Baby" was a strange label - perhaps a long standing tag - for a child of four, but this child was my mother, Marjory Barlow! The report of the floral tributes is helpful in another respect because if makes reference to the Sergeant-Major's three other grandchildren, Geraldine, Alan and Gordon. I met Gordon sometime in the 1950s. I remember he gave me my first ride on a motorcycle and that he lived and worked in one of the former East African colonies. Both my brother and I remember Geraldine being referred to, but we don't remember meeting her. Alan we had never heard of.

---

* Flora Thompson, the author of the celebrated story of late 19th century country life, Lark Rise to Candleford, spent her working life in the Post Office. In the early part of her career she worked in a hamlet Post Office somewhat in character with Sydling St Nicholas, where after training she was sometimes left in charge of the telegraph machine.

Among its own reportage of the event the *Bury Guardian* added:-

> "Popular sympathy manifested itself in a very large degree at the funeral of the late Sergeant-Major Ash...   Shortly before quarter to two the people began to line up about the Peel Monument* and in the Market Place generally, and as the time drew near for the funeral cortege to arrive there was a plentiful sprinkling of khaki among the people, due principally to the number of men who are at home on leave from Southport on account of Inoculation. An impressive spectacle was presented by the appearance of the cortege.
> During the procession from the house in School Brow to the Parish Church, the men of the 5th Battalion the Lancashire Fusiliers (2nd Reserve)... lined up ... They numbered in round figures about 500, half of them in uniform, and half still in mufti. At the... [cemetery] there was also a large public demonstration, the people thronging the drives adjacent to the situation of the grave. Three volleys were fired... Bayonets were fixed."

The extent and scope of the reporting is remarkable for its detail and it has a certain out of date feel. In spite of the point-by-point coverage neither of the newspapers report how many of the "friends and neighbours" from the Nob Inn attended the funeral, or indeed whether there was anyone from the Grey Mare Hotel - the military character seems to have been the focus.

From the above, the reader will see how valuable was the microfilm archive of the *Bury Times.* When it was first developed, the technology was a revolutionary method of storing an image at a reduction in size and weight, which in its day was of very large proportion. This reduction is, of course, nuga-tory compared with digital storage capacities. Future generations of researchers may have indexed newspapers and the ability to search for "keywords" in year-loads of newspapers in mere seconds. Such a facility, if it existed, may have pro-duced for me the 'Sergeant-Major shoots raging bull' story (see Chapter 2) but, alas, without some reasonable fix on time of an event, the trawl through micro-film archives is a task only for the infatuated.** Only some few weeks into this tale my wife had said to me earnestly *"You mustn't get obsessed with this research you are doing".* She was far too late with her warning for I could offer no other reply than *"What do you mean 'obsessed'? I already am!"* But to return to the micro-film archive, that it is available to the public is, to me, a matter of great satisfac-tion and it is evident from the above how it yielded a harvest of wonderful revelations of titanic proportion.

Yet it frightens me. It frightens me whenever I recall how two gems might so easily have been missed (one in my family's terms being a crown jewel) if I had

---

* This is the monument to Bury's most famous son, Sir Robert Peel who was the first Prime Minister to come from an industrial family; the monument is near the Parish Church.
** I had actually joined these ranks but not to the extent of being willing to look through 13 years of newspaper microfilm records for a story which might not have been there.

not gone back over the same ground looking again at what I had already reviewed on microfilm. The first of these I found two months later when reviewing the hard copy original *Bury Times* issue of 13 March 1915, stored by the British Library newspaper collection in Colindale, North London. As I turned the pages of this 86 year old newspaper looking for the piece I knew already was there, I alighted, through serendipity, on the following editorial which I had not previously noticed, for when searching on microfilm it is all too easy to miss what you are not looking for.

"An honourable career came to an end with the death of Sergeant-Major Ash on Monday [8 March 1915]... The Sergeant-Major was of fine presence - a typical Guardsman... He had the true soldier's respect for the King's Commission, and nothing could exceed the promptness with which he accorded it the full measure of honour. He was ever a courteous and obliging Sergeant-Major... His return to military duties [on the outbreak of the Great War in August 1914] after more than seven years of retirement was probably in accordance with his own wishes as it undoubtedly was in accordance with his sense of duty. The scene at his funeral...was... one such as we seldom witness even at interments at which full military honours are accorded."
Editorial: Bury Times, 13 March 1915.

This was amazing. I had already been much more than just agreeably surprised at how much coverage the Sergeant-Major's death and funeral had been given. It had pleased me to read the Brigade Commander's tribute but at the back of one's mind is always the knowledge that the hidden wiring of a bureaucracy causes it to eulogise on cue, but the editorial was different. What caused that editor to pick up the pen and write such a spontaneous and generous tribute? No one would have commented if it had not been published - its non-existence would have passed unremarked. Those who read the 1500 or so words which had already been written reporting his death and his funeral would have been stimulated into whatever emotions their consciousness directed, and they would have been moved, more or less, by the memory of the Sergeant-Major according to how well or whether they knew him. But the editor wasn't satisfied. He wanted more!

The *Bury Guardian* was not to be outdone. Its editorial on 13 March read:-

"It was with deep regret that we recorded the death of Sergeant-Major Ash. He was a man of wide military experience and one who was held in the highest regard by officers and men of the 1st Volunteer Battalion.... and since his rejoining the force he has earned for himself the same popularity in the... Territorials. Sergeant-Major Ash was a soldier, and this simple definition possesses a wealth of meaning. He knew his work - he had a capacity for creating the best spirit among the mess, for had he occasion to be displeased he never showed any deep feeling of vexation. He had seen service in Egypt, but Egyptian life had no great attraction for him, as the climate was so intensely hot in the summer months."

I started this account by noting the high esteem in which the Sergeant-Major was held by his family. Clearly, the reader should now be able to accept that this was no puffed up sentiment conveniently enlarged by the telling. Neither can it be written off as the natural warmth of memory of a daughter, my grandmother, for her father. This esteem, it was now becoming clear to me, was not at all exaggerated; on the contrary it is understated. The reader must understand that none of what I write, save the esteem, was handed down. There were no scrapbooks, no letters, no cuttings, and no photographs - only the clock! As I have already written, if this story had never emerged it would have been a travesty.

But there was yet more - more on the microfilm that I might have missed if I had not gone over the same ground again as I had covered during my first visit to Bury. The second time I scrolled in to the report on the Sergeant-Major's funeral, with whatever rationale I cannot say other than a hunting instinct, something new commanded my gaze. The beacon words were 'SERGEANT-MAJOR ASH'. As I focused I realised I was looking at the advert for a picture-house (cinema) which displayed the films which would be shown next week, and there at the bottom the advert read *"a very fine film showing the FUNERAL OF SERGEANT-MAJOR ASH will be shown today... at all performances."* I was stunned. A cataract of emotions and reactions followed as the enormity of this serendipity broke upon me. A film had been made - it seemed incredible - of my grandfather's funeral.

I had first to pinch myself to be reminded that cinemas existed at all in 1915. But there it was, the Art Picture Hall (the purpose built building still stands in Knowsley Street, Bury) with the advert for its various showings next week not looking greatly different from their modern equivalent. The concept of the newsreel does not exist no, of course, forced into its demise by television. I remember them well enough from my childhood but the concept of local news on newsreel did not exist for me. In the 1950s they were all corporately made for a homogeneous national audience. But here was local news being presented on screen almost as fresh as fish from the sea. The event (the funeral) took place on Wednesday afternoon - the advert appeared in the Saturday edition of the *Bury Times*. Some local film maker had been hard at work between these times because his film was first shown that very day, and it was my great-grandfather's funeral!

It seems incredible even as I write. All I had three months earlier was his clock and the inscription on it, and from that fragment I had found out so much. Of course, the extent of what I had found out brought joy, but it was touched by a continuing sense of anger that the story had been denied my brother and I.

When I have told friends and acquaintances this part of the story, they have invariably said something like "Oh, how amazing! Was he famous?" If we mean "famous" in the sense of being an historical figure or even a footnote to history, then I don't think he was famous. I say this in spite of his funeral being attended by "thousands". I think there can be no doubt he was popular and much liked. The evidence exists to assert that he was held in high regard.

He was certainly well known - he had run two pubs and so far as the Army in Bury is concerned his name would have been on every lip - he would have been known by every officer, every squaddy and NCO in the Battalion, past and present and probably in other battalions of the regiment. It should be remembered too that although he had been retired (from his first service) for eight years, very many soldiers would have passed through his hands. As generation after generation of squaddies came and went they would all remember the Sergeant-Major. If he were popular and well liked there might be thousands of ex-soldiers who would have remembered him and who wanted to be at his funeral. And remember, we are in Bury, which was the depot town of the Lancashiire Fusiliers; many of Sergeant-Major Ash's ex-soldiers would be local men.

I have put these points to those people with whom I have discussed the story with more or less success in advancing the more modest explanation of how 'thousands' came to be at his funeral. It must also be recalled, and properly weighed, that the country was just emerging from the first winter of a war whose awfulness was beginning to strike on the consciousness of its people. Stalemate had set in on the Western Front. The 1st Battalion, Lancashire Fusiliers were just about to sail as part of the Fusilier Brigade in the crack 29th Division on their way, as it turned out to Gallipoli. Expectation about where this division was to be posted was rife. In all these circumstances I advance the theory that in a military town, with so many of its sons in uniform in wartime, a good military funeral could be like a draught of tonic to warm the souls which was hearing precious little on which to keep cheerful. Or maybe many hearts were full of foreboding and the death of a popular man gave vent to their sorrow. I think it was not the fame of the man, but the volume of kindly remembrances, and this is no small point - the social climate in the times in which he died - which account for the thousands who attended his funeral.

These thoughts, however, were all assembled later when I had had a chance to reflect on the enormity of what I had discovered on my first trip back to Bury. At the time I was thinking more of my desire to find the film of the Sergeant-Major's funeral and the seeming hopelessness of the task *"How do you start?"* I asked myself. *"How do you start to look for a newsreel film shown in a local cinema 86 years ago?"* To say it was daunting was not enough. I could only just restrain the feeling of hopelessness. Succeeding in this restraint I nevertheless had a vision of a mission that might take a year and may even end in failure after such a time. In the event it took only until the next day. Yes - just 36 hours - that's all it took because I was lucky!

As I have already recounted, I travelled to Bury on a Monday morning. I started at the Public Library on the Tuesday sharp at 9 o'clock for my booked time on the microfilm reader/printer. My day had started at 7.30 am communion at the Parish Church, followed by a guided tour round all the Lancashire Fusiliers memorabilia including a delightful tablet presented by the crew of *Euryalus*.

By mid-morning I had found everything I thought I was going to find on microfilm. As I walked round Bury's famous indoor market over lunchtime I was in awe of the material I had found. Later in the week when I went back to the library to say my goodbyes and give my thankyous, I remarked to a dear lady who had helped me so much with the archives that I had been very successful and that I thanked my luck. She said in reply that whatever luck I'd had was deserved because I had made the effort to come and do research on the spot. *"So many family researchers expect to do it all from their armchairs!"* she said. But it was still Tuesday. In the afternoon I went back to the Lancashire Fusilier's Museum.

On that occasion I chanced to meet a local artist, Mark Adams, who was looking to do artwork for the museum. Overhearing his conversation I wondered whether he would or could accept my commission to paint a portrait of Sergeant-Major Ash from the photograph I now had from the *Bury Times*. We discussed the difficulty of creating a good portrait from the poor image of a photograph taken off a microfilm - clearly, it was not satisfactory. The answer seemed to be to reproduce an image off the original hard copy newspaper. This would by-pass one level of reproductive degradation. But did the original hard copy exist? With this prompt I tried later that afternoon to reach the editor of the *Bury Times* , only to be told to ring back in the morning.

On Wednesday morning at about 9.30 am I rang and was put through to the Editor, Bill Allen. Somewhat in trepidation, after an attempted introduction, I asked:-

"Do you have a hard copy of the Bury Times for March 1915?"
"Yes."
"Can I have a look at it please?"
"Yes."
"Can I come round now?"
"Yes."

Forty minutes later I was standing in the lobby of the *Bury Times* office/print works looking at a huge hard back heavily bound volume of original copies of the *Bury Times*. I found the photo I was looking for which would now make it possible for a digital image to be taken to form the sketch for a portrait of the Sergeant-Major. As I was reaching this conclusion I became conscious of a young man who was taking more than a passing interest in what I was doing. Evidently, the interest in me of this *Bury Times* reporter Terry Morgan, had been engaged by his observation of a book I was carrying on Gallipoli - a subject it transpired that was of particular interest to him. He was in frequent touch with the museum on Gallipoli and other Lancashire Fusilier matters.

It didn't take long before I was explaining my mission. As I showed him the *Bury Times* piece on the Sergeant-Major's funeral there was the Art Picture Hall advert on the same page. *"How do you go about finding a film like that?"* I asked as I showed him the reference to the newsreel. It was said more rhetorically than pleadingly but before I knew what was happening he excused himself and went back into the back office, to do what I didn't speculate.

I was surprised and delighted when he came back with a few names and telephone numbers from his own database, of prominent members of the *'Bury Cine Society'*. *"They might be able to help you track it down"* he proffered. Within half an hour I was on the 'phone to the Secretary, Terry Ashworth. The question I wanted to ask seemed so absurd and so improbable that I could hardly form the words in my mouth to articulate them. I took a breath, put aside the absurdity, and said - *"I'm trying to trace a newsreel film that was shown in Bury in March 1915."*

The half expected snigger or chuckle did not come down the telephone. Instead came the unfazed reply - *"Well, we don't have anything at all of that vintage. It's too old for us but if anyone has it then it will be with the North West Film Archive."*

This, it transpired, is a film archiving organisation which, as the name implies, retains anything on film to do with north west England under the auspices of Manchester Metropolitan University in Chorlton Street, Manchester. Shortly after 12:30 pm that same day, I was on the 'phone to them. I had to 'stiffen the sinews' again to formulate and utter the question which sounded, so it seemed to the man who posed it, like an invitation to mock:- *"I am trying to trace a newsreel film that was shown in Bury in 1915."*

Getting ready to duck the impatient reply, which didn't come, I wasn't quite ready for:- *"Well, we may have it. Are you on the Internet?"* I spluttered that I did have access to it at home but that I had driven up from Surrey and couldn't access it while I was away from home. Taking pity on me, the delightful young lady said: *"OK, I'll have a look for you. It may take a couple of hours."*

Not being in a position to dictate the pace, I thanked her. I went off for my lunch. At 2:30 pm my phone rang:- *"I've found it."* the cheery voice said. *"Good God, Can I see it?"* I asked. *"Yes, come to Manchester!"* she replied.

One and a half hours later, after an intriguing journey on what started on what seemed like a train but ended as a tram trundling through the streets of Manchester, I was sitting in a studio watching a film of my great-grandfather's funeral! That fact - that amazing string of serendipitous circumstances which led to it is as hard for me to take in again as I write of the event, as it must be for the reader who takes it straight from the page. This was the Wednesday. I had only left home on the Monday armed only with hope, the inscription on *"the handsome timepiece"*, the golden snippets from the Lancashire Fusiliers and the date of the Sergeant-Major's death from the Internet! Can any reader doubt the warm inner glow I felt as I drove south the following day?

The film, which is more remarkable for its existence than its artistic merit, is barely four minutes long. Monochrome of course and it has no sub-titles. The opening frame describes it as a 'Military Funeral, Bury, 11 March 1915'.

It is only the *Bury Times* advertisement reference to it which enables it to be identified as Sergeant-Major Ash's funeral. Certainly the North West Film Archive knew nothing of the provenance of the film. That I was able to give it later, in some detail, was as welcome to them as it was pleasing to me.

How were newsreels presented in those days? It seems bizarre to have a film show where the audience is in ignorance of what is being shown! From what I have seen of silent films they had a few frames of commentary every now and again so that the audience could keep the thread. In any event the film of the funeral that survives has no commentary of any nature. The reader must suffice with my own.

The opening shot, taken from near to the front entrance of Bury Parish Church, is of two files of about 15 soldiers each slow marching round a corner past Park's Bank, wearing their flat caps and carrying their rifles 'at the reverse'. a band is following the two files of soldiers who separate to form an honour guard at the steps of the church. The soldiers' movements are somewhat undrilled, clumsy it might be said, as they formed up and dressed on the church steps, with their rifles upside down, their muzzles on a boot, heads bowed.*

As the band dissolves to the side of the road the hearse appears, drawn by two large black horses with a civilian in control on top. Two files of soldiers, who would not be thought smart at all except by their mums, accompany the hearse, and are to be the bearers. The horses are brought to a halt almost on top of the camera. The film switches to the coffin being borne up the steps into the church between the two honour-guard files, at their reverential position with heads bowed. On the coffin is a Union flag, a busby and some flowers. Looking on, a crowd many deep on the pavement and at the church steps where mothers carrying babes in arms are watching the proceedings.

The film cuts to the chief mourners going into church. A man in a top hat with a lady (the Sergeant-Major's widow and his younger son?) followed by four ladies, all in the same uniform of round-headed-feathered hat and long skirted overcoats - these are probably my spinster great aunts! The film cuts to a file of what, according to the *Bury Times* report, may be soldiers dressed in civilian clothes headed by an officer, who attempt the slow march. They are dressed universally in collar and tie, buttoned jacket and variously in a bowler hat or flat cap. A cut is made to two-abreast soldiers making a group of about 50 who slowly amble (it doesn't look like a slow march) towards the church steps where they take off their caps. The film ends in panning into the crowd, many deep, all looking glum and cheerless, as well they might in such solemn circumstances.

To my great regret the film, or at least that which remains of it, does not include the firing of three volleys over the grave at the burial. At a later date I chanced upon an 1893 drill manual in which I was able to read the then current

---

* The *Bury Guardian* used a still of this shot as a photograph in their edition of 13 March 1915.

instructions for funeral parties which read:-

"The party appointed for escort, according to the rank of the deceased, will be drawn up two deep, with opened ranks and unfixed bayonets, facing the house where the corpse is lodged. Small parties that are to march in files will be formed with the files extended at 1 side pace from each other. When the corpse is brought out, the officer commanding will proceed as follows:-

    "PRESENT - ARMS"
    "REVERSE - ARMS "

It continues:-

"The funeral service will be performed, after which, the escort will proceed as follows:-

    "ATTENTION"
    "PRESENT - ARMS"
    "SHOULDER ARMS"
    "WITH BLANK CARTRIDGES READY FIRE THREE VOLLEYS IN THE AIR"
    "PRESENT"
    "FIRE"
    "FIRE"
    "FIRE"

I wish I could have seen a film of the firing at my great-grandfather's grave.

Chapter 5

George Ash: 1858 to 1915 - Sydling St Nicholas

In the space of just a few months I had found out the whole shape of George Ash's life. He had been born the second of five children of a poor peasant family in a poor Dorset village. He finished his life as a highly respected member of his community, and of his regiment, in a northern industrial town as far removed in its economy, in its culture and in its lifestyle from his farm labouring youth as it is possible to imagine. His promotion to Sergeant-Major (the highest non-commissioned rank in the Army, and effectively the highest that the system allowed a man with neither education nor privilege) at the age of 28 gave official recognition that his life was a successful one. He may not have been rich (his estate in 1915 would have been worth some £50,000 or so in today's money) but his life was enriched by experience and achievement. Imagine ! A farm labourer's boy, served in Egypt and was later in charge of a battalion of several hundred men having served in three crack regiments, the Scots Guards, the Royal Fusiliers and, of course, the Lancashire Fusiliers.

Imagine ! A farm labourer's boy mounting a guard at Buckingham Palace, at Windsor Castle, at Dublin Castle and at the Tower of London. Imagine ! A farm labourer's boy marching through the streets of London from Wellington Barracks in Birdcage Walk to change the guard at Buckingham Palace and the Bank of England. The former is, of course, a popular tourist attraction; the daily march to change the guard at the Bank of England used to be a daily affair until traffic congestion put a stop to it in the late 1960's or 1970's; I remember seeing it as a young City worker. Was it some genetic hand down that made me stop and watch those marching Guards ? Is it some hidden wiring that compels me now, still to this day, to stand and watch drilling soldiers ? How much pride I would have had when the Scots Guards were on guard duty marching through the City of London ? Of course, if I had known when I was a boy what I know now it seems to me to be very likely that I would have chosen a military career. The fact that I didn't know, that I didn't consider joining the Army is, I suspect, the granting of my grandmother's wish (on account of her bitterness over the loss of her brother at Gallipoli) that I should not be a soldier.

But I have the Sergeant-Major's *"handsome timepiece"*, which ticks on as I write, in which to bestow my pride; no army career for me but an interest in battles. If I had joined the Army I would have wished it to have been as an officer. That is Sergeant-Major Ash's legacy. He may have started as a farm labourer but he ended working for officers and gentlemen. His children entered the middle classes. I knew four of his daughters; they were all ladies. His elder son was, as we have seen, chief clerk of the Bury Corporation Tramway.

The birth places of his eight children illustrate the itinerant life of a service family; the Tower of London, Dublin Castle, Wellington Barracks, Finsbury Barracks, Chelsea and St George's Barracks in London, Windsor and Tilbury Fort and finally Bury in 1894 where George and Lizzie Ash settled for the rest of their lives, with a short period nearby, at the Nob Inn, Little Lever.

As he spent time in Blackpool with Lizzie Ash on that final weekend of his life, what may have been in his mind ? There can be no doubt he would think of his son Vivian in Egypt: would these thoughts have extended to Gallipoli ? The military significance of The Dardanelles had been announced by the naval bombardments, of which we will hear more later; Lizzie would have to cope with the horror, as the Lancashire Fusiliers were drawn into the campaign progressively over the next few months, without her husband. Fancy, he might have thought; my lad following in my footsteps in Egypt! He would have thought of his own service in that country and the battle of Tel-el Kebir; he might have been hoping that his son would return from that country as proud and victorious as he had done 33 years earlier. He might have thought of the Nob Inn where he had only recently given up as licensee and perhaps he might have thought of his early life and how far he had come since he walked out from his Dorset home some 40 years earlier.

George Ash was born on 11 July 1858 in Sydling St Nicholas, in rolling countryside some 10 miles north of Dorchester. When I first started this account, the reader will appreciate that I did not know where it would take me. My only thoughts to begin with were of Bury. I had never heard of Sydling St Nicholas. I didn't even know that my grandmother's family had adopted Bury as their hometown; I had always assumed that they were rooted in Bury from all time. To have discovered an ancestral connection with a village of such indisputable charm was a huge bonus. I went to visit the village some three months after this story began, for no other purpose than to become acquainted with it. Now that I know how nice it is I expect that I will want to return habitually. Sydling St Nicholas lies in a short valley through which runs a clear chalk stream, which accounts for its existence. It has a chocolate box charm today; the tourist industry has more or less passed it by, served as it is only by a small number of Bed and Breakfasts and as fine a pub, the Greyhound Inn, as you will find, cheery service of quality offerings.

Over the last 200 years the population of the parish of Sydling St Nicholas has fluctuated through wide limits with a high of nearly 700 in 1861 just after George Ash was born, falling to around 350 in 1921 by which time, presumably, the secular trend of the shift away from the land had, for the greater part, run its course. The lowest census figure is 321 in 1971 and the estimated figure in March 2001 is 422.

The 1861 census shows George Ash's parents, Robert (32) and Jane Ash (29), living in Ham Cottages with Eliza (5), George (2) and Mary (3 months).

Sydling St Nicholas, nestling in its valley
(Photo courtesy of residents of Sydling)

Ham Cottage, Sydling St Nicholas, where George Ash lived 1858 to 1875.
(Photo courtesy of residents of Sydling, probably early 20th Century)

Also in the house on 15 April 1861 was Grace Marsh (19) a 'visitor' who like both Robert and Jane, as born in Dinnington, (just over 20 miles away in Somerset). "Marsh" was the maiden name of Jane Ash; Grace Marsh was probably her sister! By 1871, the children have been joined by Sarah (8) and John (4), but Eliza, who is 15 by now is missing, presumably living somewhere else probably as a domestic servant (in 1881 she re-appears unmarried at 25 and living with her parents and recorded as being in domestic service). In 1881 Emma makes her appearance aged 10. It is Emma who travelled from Dorset to Bury to attend her brother's funeral in Bury in 1915.

Robert Ash, George's father died in June 1882 at the age of 55. By the time of the 1891 census Jane, his widow, was living in Up Sydling (higher up the valley) with Emma now aged 20 and also in domestic service. Jane Ash was buried in her husband's grave in St Nicholas's churchyard in June 1909, aged 78. All the children bar Emma seem to have left Sydling by 1881 and none of them was married in the village church. The evidence for this is the parish register. Curiously the baptisms register shows neither George nor Emma Ash as having been baptised. Unless this was done elsewhere (and I can't imagine how it would have been) this leaves hanging in the air why three of the Ash children were baptised and two were not!

I began to wonder what life would have been like when George Ash lived at Sydling St Nicholas in the mid nineteenth century. I found several social histories to help me.

Writing about the village in a local history* two local historians say:-
"Travelling north-west along the Yeovil Road from the ancient town of Dorchester, one arrives at the hamlet of Grimstone. Then, under the railway viaduct, as through a gateway, one enters another world - the lower reaches of the Sydling Water - the entrance to the Sydling Valley."

It's true, even today the viaduct is still there and the valley has an ageless feel touched only occasionally by the motor car, farm vehicles and school buses. It is unusual in that there is an almost complete absence of any manifestation of the modern world. Yes there is a telephone kiosk but there are no shops (there is a farm shop in Up Sydling), no advertisement hoardings, no car parks, but just a church, a pub, a village stream with several branches and a waterfall and 180 or so houses, many thatched, of more or less great charm. Admittedly there is no longer a cricket green but then there is scarcely enough flat ground for one! Wherever one goes there is the ever present gurgling of the flowing streams searching their way down the valley which, lower down, provide the water for a trout farm and watercress beds. The whole village and the surrounding space is a conservation area, as well it should be. In the words of the villagers:-
"Much of the visual appeal of the village lies in the variety of period architectural features

* *An introduction to the History of Sydling St. Nicholas in Dorset* by LWG and GM Hudson: 1973

displayed by the houses. Among the flint, stone and rendered walls are many mellow brick frontages, showing Georgian sash windows and doors. Climbing roses, Boston ivy and flowering shrubs add rich colours and textures."

In Thomas Hardy's story "The Grave by the Handpost" he describes the parish boundary between Sydling St Nicholas and Maiden Newton, a bigger village in the adjacent valley only some three and a half miles away, as: *"The lovely monotonous old highway...which runs straight...on the foundation of the Roman Road".* Evidently the Romans left no other mark. There is a Doomsday Book reference which post-dates a Saxon settlement; the valley sides are patterned with the earthworks of Iron Age field systems of enclosures and Medieval strips called *"lynchets".*

Parts of the church are very old (500 years) on a site that is probably Saxon. It has a clock with no face but which has an energetic stirring as it strikes the hour, producing a mechanical performance, which demands a temporary halt in any proceedings that may be taking place in the church at the time. In George Ash's time, when the society of Sydling was one of poor land-labouring families, it is doubtful if there were many homes that had their own clock. The hour strikes of St Nicholas's clock would have marked the passage of time and conducted the rythms of the working day of the men in the fields and their wives at home. The clock dates from 1593 and evidently it is the second oldest of its kind in England.

Cromwell is blamed for the absence of stained glass in the church windows, but this absence is, in fact, an unusual blessing! The result of plain glazing is that it has become "a church with a view". On a sunny summer evening the view of the eastern side of the valley makes Evensong an unusually joyous occasion where, through the glazing above the altar, the yellowing beams of late sunlight can be seen falling on the hills, with their grazing sheep, which run north to south to the east of the village. In 1966 the church was used in the filming of Thomas Hardy's novel *"Far from the madding crowd"* which starred Alan Bates and Julie Christie.

During the Middle Ages the village belonged to Milton Abbey but after the Dissolution of the Monasteries under Henry VIII, the land was confiscated and then sold in its virtual entirety to Winchester College who then held it continuously for 400 years. For hundreds of years it seems that nothing much changed. In a certain sense the village has suffered from the absence of the benign influence of the squire! Since the sixteenth century until the 1960's practically the whole village was under the control of an absentee landlord who would have been more interested in collecting rents than in taking any paternalistic view of stewardship. Due to the lack of wealth and because the whole village was in a single ownership, change was very slow. In its time, and certainly in George Ash's time, Sydling St Nicholas had been a poor village for poor people. In spite of the disposal programme commenced by the College in the1960's, the village has emerged into the modern world with a rare integrity now made enduring, happily, because of its conservation area status. It is a little time warp, which is a tribute to the modern way of attributing an aesthetic valuation of buildings and places from the past that are as much for the future as they were for the past. Anyway, Sydling St. Nicholas has been captured and any change that takes place in the future will, more or less, be sympathetic and slow. Sydling's snail-like pace of change compared with other nuclear villages, which have, through time, been in diverse private ownerships, is set to continue.

But what might life have been like for George Ash when he lived there from 1858 to 1875? It was probably unchanged for the best part of a thousand years and unchangeable until the arrival of the internal combustion engine. As George Ash walked out one August morning in 1875 on his way to a new life in the Army it is easy to draw the parallel with Laurie Lee, the celebrated poet, essayist and writer. Like George Ash, Laurie Lee as recounted in his autobiographic *"As I Walked Out One Midsummer Morning"* left his country village at the age of 19 (in his case) never to return, but to go on to a life of fame and fortune through his literary talent. Laurie Lee walked from Gloucester to London (and ultimately across Spain) as he set out on that August day in 1933 on his journey through life.

Buses now run once a day between Sydling and Dorchester and Sherborne with an extra service on Wednesdays and Saturdays. When George Ash set out in 1875 on his journey through life he would have kissed his mother 'goodbye' at the garden gate of Ham Cottages and probably walked over the hill to the railway station at Maiden Newton some two and a half miles away to catch a train to Dorchester. The railway connecting Weymouth and Yeovil and which runs through the next valley to the west, opened in January 1857, the year before he was born. Or, even more likely, he would have walked the mere 10 miles to the recruiting office in Dorchester.

George Ash didn't achieve the fortune or fame of Laurie Lee but he was sufficiently well known and liked in Bury for '*thousands*' to watch his funeral procession; not many people achieve this mark of an acknowledgement of their passing. For a peasant boy to have achieved this is to me quite astonishing!

Laurie Lee is useful in trying to understand what George Ash left behind when he left Sydling St Nicholas in 1875. Laurie Lee immortalised his autobiographic* account of his childhood life in Shad, a village in a Gloucestershire valley, in which he writes:

"The last days of my childhood were also the last days of the village".

He lived two generations later than George Ash but what he describes of his valley is probably the image of George Ash's valley.

"I belonged to that generation which saw.... the end of a thousand years' life."
"Myself, my family.... were born in a world of silence; a world of hard work and necessary patience, of backs bent to the ground, hands managing the crops, of waiting on weather

---

* *Cider with Rosie* by Laurie Lee: 1959

The School, Sydling St Nicholas, attended by George Ash, now converted to a private house.
(Author's Photo, 2001)

The Waterfall opposite Ham Farm, Sydling St Nicholas. The lady in the photograph is Sarah Newbury who was about the same age as Emma Ash and would certainly have known the Ash family.
(Photo courtesy of the residents of Sydling. Probably early twentieth century)

and growth; of villages like ships in the empty landscapes and the long walking distances between them; of white narrow roads, rutted by hooves and cart-wheels, innocent of oil and petrol, down which people passed rarely, and almost never for pleasure, and the horse was the fastest thing moving. Man and horse were all the power we had - abetted by levers and pulleys. But the horse was king, and almost everything grew around him - fodder, smithies, stables, paddocks, distances and the rhythm of our days. His eight miles an hour was the limit of our movement, as it had been since the time of the Romans."

Another author, Flora Thompson, has given us another account of rural village life even closer to George Ash's time*. She describes her own Oxforshire village in the 1880's (George Ash left Sydling in 1875) as being:

"... largely self supporting. Every household grew its own vegetables, produced its new laid eggs and cured its own bacon. Jams and jellies were made at home as a matter of course. Most gardens had a row of beehives. ...Even the poor enjoyed a rough plenty."

Flora Thompson's account tells us that George Ash's father's life would have been, without any suggestion of paradox, both hard and contented. The farmers were always willing to employ an extra hand. Labour was lavishly used for it was cheap and the land was well tilled. On arriving early for work the men, probably dressed in the traditional smock-frock topped by a round black felt hat, would lead out their teams of horses and file off to the field where their day's work was to be done:

"If it rained, they donned sacks, split upon one side, to form a hood and cloak combined. If it was frosty, they blew upon their nails and thumped their arms across their chest to warm them. If they felt hungry after their bread-and-lard breakfast, they would pare a turnip and munch it..."

When they had finished in the fields, this was not the end of the day for the farmlabourer ! Flora Thompson tells us that:-

"On light evenings, after their tea-supper, the men worked for an hour or two in their gardens or allotments. They were first-class gardeners and it was their pride to have the earliest and best of the different kinds of vegetables."

In Flora Thompson's 1880's Oxfordshire

"They still spoke the dialect... the syllables were slurred, and words were run together, as'brenbu'er' for bread and butter. They had hundreds of proverbs and sayings and

---

Lark Rise to Candleford, a trilogy by Flora Thompson: 1945

their talk was stiff with simile. Nothing was simply hot, cold or coloured; it was "hot as hell," "cold as ice," or "yellow as a guinea"... one might be "mad as a bull." or "poor as a rat." "sick as a dog," "hoarse as a crow," "as ugly as sin"... or "stinking with pride."

This gives us something of the rural life that George Ash left behind him as he walked out of the Sydling valley in August 1875 at the age of 17. Laurie Lee's account continues:-

"the church ... never appeared more powerful. Its confident bell rang out each Sunday; the village heard it, asked no questions, put on satin and serge (and) filed into the pews, bobbed and nodded, frowned at its children, crouched and prayed, and sat in blank rows or jerkily slept while the curate reeled off those sermons which he had hired from the ecclesiastical library."

"Sunday, far from being a day of rest, was in some ways tougher than a weekday. On that one day in seven - having bathed the night before - we were clean, wore our best and ate meat. But in the packed congregation solemnity ruled. There was power, lamentation, full-throated singing, heavy prayers and public repentance. From our seats in the choir we watched the year turn - Christmas, Easter and Whitsun ... and prayers for rain, the Church following the plough very closely. Harvest Festival perhaps was the one we liked best, the one that came the nearest to home."

So wrote Laurie Lee. The present day villagers of Sydling St Nicholas have produced a charming village book* to describe life in the village during the millennium year 2000. In it Mrs Jean Morris (born 1921) recalls how hard life and work of a farm worker used to be. We can be certain it was much the same in George Ash's day.

This is what she says of the life of a farm labourer:

"There was no lifting machinery; the entire day would be spent walking and holding a heavy jolting plough behind a pair of horses or on a freezing day moving hurdles to make new enclosures for sheep. His wages were low, his cottage often damp with no electricity or water. His day started by bringing in water from the village pump. His garden was precious to him as home grown vegetables were vital for survival. On Sundays church attendance was obligatory.

His leather boots were a large expenditure but an overcoat was too expensive so he wore hessian sacks over his shoulders in bad weather.

The village school taught him to read and write, then at 14 he was sent out to work, nearly always on the farm where he toiled for the rest of his life. He knew nothing else and did not even know how to be discontented."

---

*   *Sydling St Nicholas. A Year in the Life of a Dorset Village,* produced by the Sydling Help and Relief Project Committee: 2000.

We can be certain about the dampness! From the inception of the Parish Council in Sydling in 1894 there has been concern about flooding. With the streams fed by springs, rainfall of any unusual quantity brings an extra volume, which puts part of the village at risk.

Much of what we are told in these accounts is confirmed in an evocative monograph* written by one of today's Sydling residents, Jack Durden. He wrote the little book, he tells us, so that his children could have some idea of what life was like in a small village in the 1930's. He spent his childhood in Mill House, now sadly demolished. By 1881 the Ash family had moved within Sydling from Ham Cottages to an address which, in the census looks like '*Mill (xxxxx) Houses*' with the middle word not being discernable. It is tempting to assert that this is the same house as Jack Durden lived in 50 years later but the evidence does not give reliable support for this. Nevertheless, if you take away bicycles and the bus from his account it seems that life in Sydling two generations earlier would have been much the same for George Ash as it was for Jack Durden. The evidence of others about the rustic life confirms Jack's claim:-

"Life was much harder than the present day. No great fortunes were made yet most villagers seemed to be more contented than they have ever been in my lifetime (since). *Perhaps this was because of the simplicity of life in those days."*

Jack Durden tells us that:-

*"The whole community had some connection with the land**. Split into small units the land was farmed as family businesses."* (It is doubtful that the Ash family did much else but labour on other people's land). *"It was said that nearly all the inhabitants were related in some way. The village boasted two shops, a bakery, a carpenter and a blacksmith's shop (whose distinctive sound and smell we experienced every day)...and of course our very own school, public house, church and chapel. It could be said we were self sufficient in every way. Milk was delivered to the door by a local farm. Firewood was delivered by the local sawmill. Everything was delivered to the door. Meat, fish* (but not before the lorries came could it be brought up fresh from Weymouth ?), *bread and all the groceries and provisions. Fresh chickens, rabbits and trout were always available."*

---

* *Village life and how to survive it* by Jack Durden: 1993

** I have studied the occupations of the fathers of all baptisms in Sydling for the 15 years from 1856 to 1870 in which time there were 254 recorded. Of these 5% were born to "single women" of whom we know nothing of the fathers; about 6% could be said to be in respect of fathers who had no connection with the land. Of all the registered baptisms, some 53% were to fathers who were farm labourers and 6% were to yeomen i.e. tenant farmers for whom the labourers worked. The rest, some 30%, were more or less skilled workers such as thatchers, shepherds, carters, blacksmiths or carpenters etc.

Jack's account confirms Laurie Lee's and other evidence about life on Sundays:

"You could never call Sunday a dull day. We would be taken to church. The church bells would summon us all for morning service where we all sat in the family pew. The afternoon was Sunday School. In the evening the bells would summon us once more for the last service of the day. When there was a vacancy, the young boys would be recruited to sing in the choir. Religion played no small part in our education. Every morning, at the start of school, the vicar would cross the road from the vicarage to read a passage from the Bible and afterwards he would explain the meaning".

This would be the same school building (remaining still but now in residential use) attended by George Ash and his siblings.

According to the census returns for 1851 and 1861, the Ash family lived in one of the four Ham Cottages standing today albeit with ground floor extensions to give some extra space, and all combined to make one home. These would have been farm labourer's cottages and the name suggests that they would have worked on the nearby Ham Farm. A beautifully illustrated village history* has an old photograph of a postman walking across the footbridge delivering mail to Ham Farm -this would have been an image seen more or less daily by George Ash.

In *Lark Rise to Candleford* Flora Thompson tells us that:

"Some of the cottages had two bedrooms, others only one, in which case it had to be divided by a screen or curtain to accommodate parents and children. Often the big boys of a family slept downstairs, or were put to sleep in the second bedroom of an elderly couple whose own children were out in the world. Except at holiday time, there were no big girls to provide for, as they were all out in service". Alternatively: *"When the older boys of a family began to grow up the second bedroom became the boys' room. Boys, big and little were packed into it ... often, it was a tight fit... and girls still at home had to sleep in the parent's room... When the girl's came home from service for their summer holiday, it was the custom for the father to sleep downstairs so that the girl might share her mother's bed..."* Some families were much bigger than the Ash's: *"... for children swarmed, eight, ten or even more in some families, and although they were seldom all at home together, the eldest often being married before the youngest was born, beds ...were often so closely packed that the inmates had to climb over one bed to get into another."*

As for downstairs:

"in a room which was kitchen, living room, nursery, wash house combined, some women would contrive to make a pleasant, attractive looking home. A well-whitened

---

* *Sydling St Nicholas: Glimpses of its History,* Edited by Sheila Philips: 1993

St Nicholas's Church, Sydling, Dorset: as seen in the film *'Far from the Madding Crowd.'*
(Author's photo.　2002)

One of the delightful chalk streams of Sydling St Nicholas.　　　(Author's photo.　2002)

hearth, a home-made rag rug in bright colours, and a few geraniums on the windowsill would cost nothing, but make a great difference to the general effect." Not everyone went in for flowers, evidently... *"But they did at least, believe in cleaning up their houses once a day, for public opinion demanded that of them. There were plenty of bare, comfortless homes... , but there was not one really dirty one. The morning cleaning proceeded to the accompaniment of neighbourly greetings, and shouting across garden and fences, for the first sound of the banging of mats was a signal for others to bring out theirs..."*

The only sanitary arrangement known in the village of Flora Thompson in the 1880's was: *"... housed... at the bottom of the garden. It was not even an earth closet; but merely a deep pit with a seat over it, the half yearly emptying of which caused every door and window in the vicinity to be sealed."* She laments the inability to seal the chimneys ! In her *'privy'* there were a succession of pictures cut from the newspapers. One she mentions is the bombardment of Alexandria in 1882. As we shall see this episode has an eerie connection with George Ash, who fought in the Egyptian campaign in that year, and, even more remotely, with his son in Gallipoli.

A recurring theme of Flora Thompson's account is the endemic poverty of the farm labourer and his family. Everything, bar food, was scarce through lack of money to buy it. This is not to say that it was an unhappy life - far from it as Jack Durden tells us, they didn't know how to be discontented. But, says Flora Thompson, the money was tight:

"As soon as a mother had even one daughter in service, the strain upon herself slackened a little. Not only was there... one pair of feet less to be shod, and a tiny space left free in the cramped sleeping quarters; but, every month, when the girl received her wages, a shilling or more would be sent to 'our Mum'. And as the wages increased the mother's portion grew larger."

Flora Thompson continues:

"Although the mothers were, naturally, grateful to and fond of their daughters, their boys, who were always at home and whose money barely paid their keep, seemed always to come first with them. If there was any inconvenience, it must not fall on the boys; if there were a limited quantity of anything, the boys must still have their full share... "

It would be another 100 years or so before this instinct became inappropriate.

As I write about George Ash's life in Sydling St Nicholas, I can't escape dwelling on the contrast he must have reflected on throughout his soldier's life between the simple life he left behind, but which was continued by his mother and father and his siblings. George Ash had marched through Cairo, he had marched through London; he had mounted guards at Buckingham Palace and now, in the final week-end of his life he was in Blackpool, the playground of the grimy Lancashire cotton towns and other industrial revolution settlements which granted no concession to the idyllic situation that was Sydling St Nicholas (then, and even now) described by Jack Durden as:-

"A lovely old village nestling in a valley surrounded by hills where I was to spend many a happy hour ... it was a very pretty village in those days. The waterfall at the side of Mill House was crystal clear and the pond below it full of large brown trout."

This pond below the waterfall can be seen in the illustration on page 54 where Jack Durden's grandmother, Sarah Newbury, can be seen by the pool. Jack tells us that:-

"I could always make pocket money from the stream that ran through the village. I seemed to have been born with the art of tickling trout. It was an unwritten law that they could be harvested by the local children! Visitors to the village could not understand that trout could be caught by hand, so I gave many a disbeliever a demonstration in the art of 'tickling".

According to Jack Durden's account he was evidently a keen observer of nature. he tells us:-

"The kingfisher could be seen at work nearby. Yellow wagtails nested in the old flint wall that surrounded the garden of Mill House. All farm hedges were laid by hand, keeping them tight and compact, making them ideal nesting places for birds. Large elm trees (now diseased and gone) *grew in these hedges giving plenty of shade for the cattle on hot summer days. In the corner of the larger fields were the hayricks with their thatched tops, a monument to the hard work that put them there."*

As with Laurie Lee's account, Jack tells us that:-

"There was always plenty of cider around at hay-making time when we would all join in to help."

There is one respect, however, in which we must beware of idealising life in Sydling St Nicholas in the 1930's let alone in mid-Victorian times. Jack Durden did not know electricity in the home or main drainage until 1950. Flooding and dampness was, as we have already seen, an endemic problem in the village. Jack tells us that in winter he had to help pull up and stack beet from the fields:-

"This was a back-breaking and hand freezing job that I was not too keen on!"

A poor family like the Ash's would have had a tough time in the long winter nights. If it could be afforded there might be a fire, but precious little light would be available. According to Flora Thompson:

"... the adult male population gathered every evening in the pub to sip its half pints, drop by drop, to make them last. It was an innocent gathering. None of them got drunk; they had not money enough ... To spend the evenings there was indeed, as the men argued, a saving, for, with no man in the house, the fire at home could be let lie down and the rest of the family could go to bed when the room got cold."

A hard life in the Army may have provided a much more certain existence than that of a farm labourer. According to Flora Thompson in the 1880's it was quite common for a boy to go off for a bit of soldiering.

"At that time boys of a roving disposition who wanted to see a bit of the world before settling down went into the Army. Nearly every family in the hamlet had its soldier son or uncle or cousin, and it was a common sight to see a scarlet coat ..."

After their army service, most of the young men returned and took up the old life on the land. That George Ash didn't return to the land is probably explained by his fast promotion.

George Ash left behind farm labouring for ever; goodness knows what sort of accent he retained against the cosmopolitan tongues of his mates in London in the Scots Guards. Even more bizarre is the thought of his speech against the dialect* of the ordinary soldier from Bury or thereabouts in the Lancashire Fusiliers! But leave Dorset he did; whether he saw his Mum again isn't recorded. We have seen that his sister Emma was sufficiently compelled to make the almost epic journey from Dorset to Bury for his funeral. His other sisters were no doubt formerly or still in service (those times were to change for ever in the Great War now in the early stages of its permanent destruction of the old way of life). On that March 1915 day, George Ash had only distant memories of that English village life on the land. He was a soldier again training the young Lancashire men to fight in the early stages of a war whose awfulness was soon to be manifested in the agony which could not yet be imagined and which was to scar his adopted town of Bury with a wound the pain of which, by the memories of my grandmother's bitterness, I am the testament of its durability, four generations on!

---

* This wasn't the only problem with dialect. I am told by a junior officer who served with the Lancashire Fusiliers that many a young officer, trained at Sandhurst and not from Lancashire, would have great difficulty with the men who would converse together in their Lancashire dialect, and be unable to comprehend them.

Flora Thompson published the first part of her trilogy as *Lark Rise* in 1939. I don't know if my grandmother read it. I suspect not but if she had I have no doubt that the last paragraph would have dissolved her to tears as it made me gasp myself as I read its tender words:

"and all the time the boys were being born or growing up in the parish (in the 1880's as was my grandmother), *expecting to follow the plough all their lives, or at most, to do a little mild soldiering. Gallipoli ...? Ypres ...? What did they know of such places? But they were to know them, and when the time came they did not flinch. Eleven out of that tiny community never came back again. A brass plate on the wall of the church ... is engraved with their names. A double column, five names long, then, last and alone, the name of Edmond."*

Like Cissie Barlow, my grandmother, Flora Thompson lost her brother to the Great War.

Chapter 6

George Ash: 1858 to 1915 - Egypt 1882

All thoughts of Gallipoli were to be in the future on that final weekend of George Ash's life in Blackpool. While taking the bracing air on the North Shore, Lizzie on his arm, George Ash is unlikely to have applied his military mind beyond the prospect of skirmishes, or battles in defence of the Suez Canal which was the principal concern of the garrison troops in Egypt where his son, Private George Vivian Ash was serving. It would be another six weeks before the question on every lip in Bury would be: where *is* Gallipoli?

As he wondered what lay ahead for his son he would have reflected on his own Egyptian experiences in the 1882 campaign: sailing up the Canal to Ismailia; a brilliant plan, masterful execution, a concentration of force, superior weapons, and a complete victory with few casualties: I only have to write this to be grateful, in a sense, that George Ash was spared knowledge of the ignoble leadership at Gallipoli and human catastrophe that was soon to break the hearts of Bury folk. Taking on the Turks in their homeland was not to be a comparable fight with taking on an Egyptian rebel army in their homeland 33 years earlier. It was not just the change brought about by the development of magazine loaded rifles and automatic machine weapons (dramatic though that had been) in the intervening period: the quality of generalship in the Egyptian campaign was peerless. Moreover, the Turks, with their German training and commanders knew a thing or two more than the Egyptian rebels about defensive fighting, and it might be said, a lot more about dying for their cause too!

The whole seventy-five year history of British involvement with Egypt begins and ends with Suez. Before the Canal was built by French initiative and opened in 1869, Egypt was of no special interest to Britain. Certainly, she had been keen enough to see the end of Napoleon's occupation eighty years earlier but lately a mutual French and British interest lay in ensuring that the vacuum created by the decline of the Ottoman Empire (including Egypt) did not jeopardise political stability in the canal zone. This interest in the Suez Canal led to the military involvement of Britain in Egyptian affairs from 1882 until 1956 with only a brief pause between her part withdrawal in 1947 and the 'ill-judged' Anglo-French and Israeli conspiracy which led to the 1956 Suez invasion and an ignominious withdrawal. But, as with the Dardanelles, strategic waterways such as Suez attract an inexorable need among nations to control them. The Suez Canal had to be defended in the Great War; it had to be defended in the Second World War too. It was when he took over as Commander-in-Chief of the Eighth Army, which had retreated across North Africa to its latest defensive position, that General Montgomery told his officers, at which they did not flinch: *"The defence of Egypt lies here at Alamein ... What's the use of digging trenches in the Delta? ... If we lose this position we lose Egypt ... Here we will stand and fight ... If we can't stay here alive, then let us stay here dead."*

Famously, Montgomery won his set piece battle at El Alamein. *"The bad times are over"* he had told his officers. His troops were told that they were going to defeat the enemy or die in the battle. As we will see in the following chapters, the Turks at Gallipoli had the same idea. But we are ahead of ourselves. The Egyptian campaign of 1882 had no parallel with the later defences of or aggression against Egypt other than the strategic imperative (or in the case of the 1956 debacle) an imagined strategic imperative. Curiously, the 1882 campaign in which George Ash served is much more comparable to a recent expedition. The opening two paragraphs of most readable short account of the 1882 campaign and the Battle of Tel El-Kebir* are most illuminating.

"When, in 1882, Lieutenant-General Sir Garnet Wolseley led a British military expedition to Egypt, fought and deposed the dictator Arabi Pasha and restored the country to the Khedive, it foreshadowed events of exactly one hundred years later when a British taskforce went out to the Falkland Islands, conquered the troops of an Argentinian dictator, Galteri, and returned the islands to British sovereignty. Separated by a century, both armies left with emotional dockside farewells and returned to Victory processions through London and public investitures by the respective Queens - all in best Victorian style.

The Egyptian War of 1882 and the South Atlantic Campaign of 1982 have much in common and bear some remarkable similarities, not least being that, from the moment of landing until the cessation of hostilities, both lasted exactly four and a half weeks. Both stretched the resources of the British Army, causing each expedition to be formed of 'crack' Regular regiments not normally used for such purposes."

It is ironic to read in the Illustrated London News (July 1882):

"... England has very few soldiers to spare. Half our regular army of 190,000 is in India and the colonies, and the lion's share of the remainder is in Ireland. ... We could not, without the undue strain of calling up our Reserves, muster more than 16,500 men of all arms for active service, and of this force a further contingent will be required to prevent Ireland from taking advantage of our embarrassment. England could not place more than 15,000 men in the field without denuding her colonies, and leaving her magazines and arsenals unprotected from those desperadoes who deal in dynamite."

As Donald Featherstone, the author of the Tel El-Kebir book, perceptively observes:-

---

* *Tel El-Kebir 1882 : Wolseley's Conquest of Egypt:* By Donald Featherstone, 1993

"Strikes a familiar chord, doesn't it?"

How much of the background to the campaign George Ash knew of or cared about can only be surmised. He was only 11 when the Suez Canal opened on 16 November 1869. It was at this point that Egyptian affairs took on an international aspect for control of Egypt was equal to control of the Canal. Access to the Canal was to be free to all nations but its importance to Britain, with its trade with India, was specially vital. The ruler of Egypt at that time, under Turkish patronage, embarked on a programme of expansion the aim of which was to achieve greater autonomy, westernisation and fast economic development.   But the expansion was too rapid and ill judged; with it came high levels of overseas debt, much of it from Britain. In 1875 (the year George Ash joined the Scots Guards) Benjamin Disraeli famously (and not altogether with authority) bought for Britain 45% of the shares in the Suez Canal Company. Even this injection of funds did not arrest the fall of the Khedive into financial ruin. In 1876 the Khedive was forced to accept British and French supervision of Egypt's financial affairs. As can be seen, although free access to the canal was in itself a vital concern, creditors in London and elsewhere were alerted to the risk of default which demanded action.

In the meanwhile, however, and not altogether surprisingly, this growing foreign intervention in Egypt's domestic affairs bred increasing internal resentment. In 1879 his son replaced the Khedive, having been deposed by the Sultan of Turkey. The deteriorating state of affairs led to a growth of a nationalist movement. In 1881 the Egyptian army mutinied; the new Khedive was powerless and early in 1882 the nationalists formed a government. The British Government proposed to France that, as the two powers most interested in the maintenance of good order in Egypt, they should intervene. The French agreed to a demonstration of an Anglo-French fleet before Alexandria. The rise of the rebel leader Arabi Pasha, who was now made Minister for War, and his inspirational leadership of his army caused alarm in Europe. In the bellicose words of the Illustrated London News:-

"Suddenly arises a military adventurer with a peculiar audacity and cunning such as oriental races alone can produce, (they are speaking of Arabi Pasha - not the Colonel Nasser of 1956!) *who has been able, step by step and in the face of a wondering world, to establish, without let or hindrance, and out of the most contemptible materials, a military despotism which threatens to depose the Khedive, and which defies, with impunity, the Western Powers and their iron-clad fleets."*

A combined British and French squadron was dispatched - Egypt's creditors wanted satisfaction. But this display of jingoism was not unrestrained. Not all were in favour of war.   Parliamentary opposition was fierce.   Moreover, suddenly, the French support was withdrawn. Britain was alone and unsure of herself. Her military resources were to be stretched.

Meanwhile, as Arabi's support grew, so his confidence rose. His engineers worked frantically to strengthen the shore forts in Alexandria where defensive earthworks were thrown up in which were mounted heavy guns. (In pausing, we may observe that these guns were from Krupps and many were commanded by Turkish officers - as Private Ash was to face in Gallipoli.) The British Fleet at anchor in Alexandria, was not disposed to tolerate this defence work going on under its nose and on 10 July 1882 an ultimatum was issued; the next day the famous bombardment of Alexandria commenced. Readers of the Illustrated London News were informed that:-

"On Tuesday morning, 11 July, after several weeks of anxious suspense, the attempts to bring about a peaceful settlement of the Egyptian difficulties were interrupted by a terrible conflict between the forts and batteries at Alexandria, under command of Arabi Pasha, and the British Naval Squadron commanded by Admiral Sir Beauchamp Seymour, occasioned by the Egyptians' conduct in persisting against repeated prohibitions, to continue their defensive and offensive warlike preparations."

Of even more interest to this account is that it was the Illustrated London News' picture of the bombardment that decorated Flora Thompson's privy as described in *Lark Rise to Candleford*. Moreover, to weld a connection between the military campaigns of father and son, the First Sea Lord at the time of Gallipoli, Lord Fisher, was in command, in 1882, of HMS Inflexible, the most powerful battleship in the Royal Navy and which took part in the bombardment of Alexandria. We will be hearing more of Lord Fisher.

The bombardment lasted until shortly after the last Egyptian gun fell silent the same day. Hopes were entertained that the naval action at Alexandria and the occupation of the city might be the end of the matter. But the British had no capacity to pursue the rebels inland. The fleet could do no more and as is always the case it proved to be a mistake to begin a naval bombardment before a military force was available to follow up its effects. As we shall see, the mistake was repeated at the Dardanelles 33 years later with bitter results before a tactical withdrawal, followed ultimately by defeat. Regaining lost prestige, and being given time to do it, Arabi withdrew his troops inland, prepared fortified positions and increased his army. Donald Featherstone tells us that:-

"Thus emboldened, he issued a proclamation declaring that 'irreconcilable war existed, between the Egyptians and the English'. and that: '... with public opinion and the press in jingoistic mood, in spite of uncertainty in Government circles through reports of uneasy foreign government attitudes and growing French hostility, British policy settled

on the dispatch of an expeditionary force to secure British interests in Egypt'. On 25 July the Queen signed the Proclamation calling out the Army Reserves."

On this day our man, Lance-Sergeant Ash was in garrison at Wellington Barracks, Birdcage Walk, London. Since December 1880 until March 1882 the 1st Battalion, Scots Guards had been on garrison duty in Dublin where the army presence was a good deal more than ceremonial! Trouble was afoot in Ireland. He had just celebrated his 24th birthday and he had been promoted three times. It was nearly seven years since he left his mother in Sydling St Nicholas. On 28 July the battalion marched from Birdcage Walk to Westminster Pier from where they were ferried to Albert Dock where they joined the 'Orient' bound for Alexandria with the Guards' Brigade on board. In addition to the Scots Guards, also on board were the 2nd Grenadiers and the 2nd Coldstreams, a total strength of 31 officers and 765 other ranks. By the 15 August two divisions, each consisting of infantry with cavalry and artillery, were on their way. The total of all troops in the campaign, from Britain, the Mediterranean and India was 40,560 officers and men.

A Royal Marine Light Infantry officer, Lieutenant W. H. Palmer, sailed a few days earlier than the Scots Guards on 27 July and wrote in his contemporary account of the campaign*, when describing the last moments before sailing:-

"For the next few minutes there was an incessant shaking of hands and bidding of farewells, and in many a brave fellow's eye a tear was seen to glisten as he bade a mute goodbye to his wife or the girl he left behind him. In one corner might be seen a mother clasping her son to her breast, as with a broken voice, she bade him good-bye and God bless you, whilst in another part of the ship a laughing crowd of brother officers were saying good-bye in their own seemingly unfeeling way, though really fearing the departure greatly." The account continues:

"Cheers loud and long rang out from all the ships in the harbour and from those who lined the beaches as we slowly steered out - our gallant men responding heartily. The last we saw of the Dockyard was a mass of people waving pocket handkerchiefs as with longing eyes they watched us disappearing. Long after the faces were indistinguishable we all remained gazing over the side at what might be our last glimpse of Old England, and the stoutest and most hardened felt, I'll warrant, a rising in his throat as the land gradually disappeared, leaving all we loved and cared for behind."

This could be from the Falkland Islands Task Force sailing, couldn't it?

---

* *Egyptian Campaign of 1882: the Journal of Lieutenant W.H.Palmer RMLI.*
Published in *The Sheet Anchor,* the magazine of the Royal Marines History Society.

The Scots Guards embarking at Westminster Bridge on 30 July 1892 en route for Tilbury and then Egypt - The Illustrated London News 5 August 1882.

(Courtesy Illustrated London News Picture Library)

As Lieutenant Palmer reminds us, men are not naturally of a despondent nature and soon the talk and laughter was as light as ever and they were eager to get to grips with the rebels. Four days later they called in at Gibralter. After leaving next day, they arrived in Malta after a further five days.

His account continues:-

"(We found, after 12 days sailing from England) ... *our longed for haven of Alexandria ... where we ... learnt that there had been a sharp skirmish on 4 August ... I drove round Alexandria ... and saw the ruins of what must have been a magnificent city. We also visited the outposts and had a glimpse of the enemy in the distance ... We were to receive a great disappointment here as, instead of landing, we were ordered to proceed to Port Said."*

This was to be part of a great outflanking manoeuvre by Sir Garnet Wolsey, the Commander-in-Chief who was, two years later, in command of the celebrated, but unsuccessful relief of General Gordon in Khartoum.

The Scots Guards arrived in Alexandria on the *Orient* on 12 August, their journey from Tilbury having taken 17 days (compared with 12 for the Royal Marines sailing from Portsmouth). Major-General HRH the Duke of Connaught was on board; he commanded the Guards Brigade which was assembling some four miles outside Alexandria and from where Arabi's forces could be observed. Sir Garnet Wolsey reached Alexandria three days later on 15 August and proceeded to implement a plan, which he had formed before leaving England.

Orders were given to embark on 18 August ostensibly to seize Aboukir, a little further up the coast (Aboukir was the site of Nelson's destruction of the French fleet in 1798.) It was not until they were at sea that they discovered that their actual destination was Ismailia, an inland port on the Suez Canal - Aboukir was a ruse.

According to the Scots Guards account:*

"Wolseley had directed the fleet to gain control of the Suez Canal, a task which was completed by August 20, and he proposed to advance on Cairo by the Sweetwater Canal, which joins the Suez Canal at Ismailia, and passed through Tel El-Kebir and the railway junction of Zagazig on its way to Cairo. The Brigade of Guards landed at Ismailia on the 22nd ... Only sufficient troops were left ... to cover Alexandria."

On 24 August a small force advanced up the Sweetwater Canal (with it forming the left flank) in a westerly direction towards Cairo as far as Tel el-Maskhuta

---

* *The History of the Scots Guards 1642 - 1914:* by Major-General Sir F. Maurice.

The Orient entering the Suez Canal en route for Ismalia with the Scots Guards on board -
The Illustrated London News, 9 September 1882.
(Courtesy Illustrated London News Picture Library)

some 20 miles from Ismailia. Finding a superior force of Egyptians nearby, the
Guards Brigade was ordered up in support. According to the Scots Guards
history:-

*"After a hot and exhausting march the brigade came on the scene just before
sundown and had its first experience of shell-fire, which did no damage. As the brigade
was cooking dinners orders came for it to extend ... outposts and the brief Egyptian
twilight had gone before the men could be got on the move. It was a difficult task to post
outposts with weary men in the pitch darkness and it was midnight before even a rough
line could be established.*

The next day it was found that the enemy had retired and (the vanguard) *troops
pushed on to Kassassin* (some 20 miles further up the canal towards Cairo), *the
Guards remaining at Tel el-Maskhuta, where they were kept busy until 9 September
repairing the railway and clearing the Canal which the Egyptians had obstructed with a
number of dams. On 28 August this work was interrupted, for Arabi made an attempt
to drive ...* (the vanguard) *from Kassassin and the Guards were again ordered up in
support."*

Evidently, the Guards were not troubled because a charge made by the Household Cavalry after sunset caused the enemy to abandon his attempts to derange the advance on Kassassin where, gradually, the forces including the Scots Guards with our man, Lance-Sergeant Ash, were concentrated. On 9 September Arabi made another attempt on the position at Kassassin but this was easily repulsed and he then withdrew into his prepared lines at Tel El-Kebir where the set piece battle, which sealed his fate, was shortly to be fought.

We have, from Lieutenant Palmer, an interesting eyewitness account of the march from Ismailia.

"By Thursday 24 August between 12,000 and 15,000 troops had been landed and the advance into the desert commenced at 2:00pm on that day, with the departure of the Guards and 60th Rifles followed at 4:00pm by our (Royal Marine) *battalion. Before marching, every officer and man was supplied with a day's ration of biscuits and bottle full of water; and each man carried 120 rounds of ammunition.*

We marched from 4:00pm ... until 12:00 at night merely halting for about half an hour two or three times. It was very heavy work as the sand was in some places up to our knees. Very glad were we when we were halted and lay down for the night ... though only four hours sleep was allowed."

This eyewitness account by Lieutenant Palmer continues:-

"We suffered greatly from thirst this day as we remained in the burning sand from 10:00am to 4:00pm, when we again marched on. The men began to fall out in great numbers and ... were left behind. Since our departure from Ismailia we had nothing to eat save the biscuits we brought with us, so we pressed on as quickly as possible ... only to find our hopes for food dashed to the ground. For about two miles the ground was simply littered with pots and pans, arms and clothing; but no food except a little salt rice and some onions ... All of us were fearfully knocked up that night."

The imperative for the advance was the occupation and holding of Kassassin Lock in order to control movements on the Sweetwater Canal which protected the left flank. Despite Egyptian attempts to dislodge it the army kept its grip. Meanwhile the Guards were kept busy repairing the railway and clearing the Canal. Back at Ismailia stores and equipment were being feverishly landed and being brought up to Kassassin by train and boat in preparation for the offensive. This feat of logistics gives graphic illustration of the brilliance of Lieutenant-General Wolsey's flanking manoeuvre to Ismailia. His whole army's need for *matériel* could be brought to the front by existing infrastructure while the Canal gave flank protection.

The Occupation of Ismailia by the Scots Guards - The Illustrated London News, 2 September 1882.
(Courtesy Illustrated London News Picture Library)

The Royal Review. The Guards at Buckingham Palace. "Three cheers for the Queen" - The Illustrated London News, 25 November 1882.
(Courtesy Illustrated London News Picture Library).

After being repulsed at Kassassin the Egyptian army retreated to its prepared lines at Tel El-Kebir. After Wolseley arrived on 11 September, a reconnaissance began the next day at dawn. Arabi had not been idle. According to Donald Featherstone's account there was:-

"... a line of entrenchments some four miles long extending from the Canal ... into the desert. At intervals along the line, connected by trenches, were gun redoubts with front and rear fields of fire."

The total force was estimated to be about 25,000 men and about 75 guns. According to Wolseley:-

"My force was about 11,000 bayonets, 2,000 sabres and 60 guns. To have attacked such a position by daylight with the troops I could place in the line would have entailed very great loss. I resolved therefore to attack before daybreak, doing the six miles that intervened between my camp and the enemy's position in the dark."

We can look to Maurice's *"History of the Scots Guards"* for a brief account of the battle:

"Sir Garnet Wolseley decided to make an attack upon them at dawn on September 13, which entailed an advance by night. This was then, for a force of the size of Wolseley's army, a novel operation, which required very careful preparation. In the event it was completely successful. The army was deployed by 11:00am on the 12th. On the right was the cavalry division, echeloned slightly back; then came the 1st Division with Graham's brigade leading and the Guards Brigade in second line. In the centre between the 1st and 2nd Divisions were forty-two guns, and on the left of the guns the 1st Division also in two lines, the Highland Brigade under Sir Archibald Allison leading. The left of the 1st Division was parallel with the railway and the Sweetwater Canal, beyond which was the Indian Contingent. The advance began at 1:30am on September 13. At 5:00am, when the first gleam of light began to appear, the Highlanders were close to the enemy's works and they at once charged and carried them. Graham's brigade assaulted a little later and by the time when the Guards reached the enemy's parapet, the battle, which had lasted barely half an hour, was over. The losses in the battalion were four men wounded, of whom one, Corporal Webster, subsequently died of wounds. Private Gaw was awarded the Distinguished Conduct Medal for remaining at duty when wounded in the head."

During the Egyptian campaign, the British Army was equipped with the Martini-Henri rifle. It had been introduced about 10 years earlier. It was a cartridge firing single shot rifle, i.e. fire and re-load. It was an accurate weapon and if faced by the British in Battalion strength, the Egyptians would have had no answer to it. We have seen already that Sergeant-Major Ash was *"The best shot in the battalion".* He would have known his way round the Martini-Henri like child's play.

Maurice's account tells us that: *"The Egyptian army lost all its guns and was completely routed at Tel El-Kebir. The cavalry division started for Cairo from the battle-field, and entered the town the next day, when Arabi surrendered his person and the citadel of Cairo."* The account given of this part of the story in Hutchinson's *History of the Nations** is much more colourful:-

"A most brilliant ride of three hundred cavalry under General French covered eighty miles (to Cairo) *by sunset, and at dusk demanded the surrender of the citadel of Cairo to the British army. Five thousand Egyptian troops sullenly filed out; a single shot would have wrecked the movement. Then the men and horses exhausted by the August day, filed in, and after three hundred had passed there was an end of them, to the extreme surprise of the Egyptians, who believed there were tens of thousands. Cairo was saved thus from fire and wreck."*

Maurice's account continues:

"On the afternoon of the 14th Sir Garnet Wolseley and the Duke of Connaught, escorted by a company of the Scots Guards ... , went by train to Cairo, where after some delay at Zagazig junction they arrived at 9:45am on the 15th.
They were followed by the rest of the battalion, which was the first infantry to enter the Egyptian capital through which it marched with pipes playing to take over the citadel from the cavalry. The rebellion was completely crushed and the Khedive entered his cap-ital in state on September 25 ... The health of the battalion in Egypt was very good. It lost altogether fifteen men, mostly from entric fever. For this little campaign the Regiment was awarded the honours for its colours of "Egypt 1882' and 'Tel El-Kebir', honours which it must be confessed were somewhat lightly won..."

On 28 September while in Cairo, our man George Ash was promoted Sergeant; just in time for the great review and march past of British troops in Cairo. According to Featherstone, there were a total of 57 officers and men killed at Tel El-Kebir and 383 wounded. What an elated feeling our man must have had as he marched through Cairo, now a sergeant in a brilliantly successful expedi-tion and only seven years since he left his peasant's smock behind in Sydling St Nicholas.

To sum up the Egyptian campaign I can do no better than quote from Featherstone:-

---

* *History of the Nations.* Ed. by Walter Hutchinson, p63.

"It was said at the time that seldom had a campaign been more completely successful or more creditable to a leader and his troops. Striking a familiar note, one writer felt that 'the war looked more like a game of Kriegsspiel than a stern reality, so careful, were the plans and calculations of Sir Garnet Wolseley, and so punctually did he carry out the scheme he had matured before leaving London'. Another military correspondent of the day said, 'He was correct almost to a day as to the date on which the campaign would be over. Not only has he finished the war triumphantly, but he has left no loose threads to be taken up. He has not merely defeated the insurgents, but he has burnt up the insurrection, leaving no pestiferous and harassing dregs behind. His strategy and tactics has been able and masterly. Instead of - as an ordinary general would have done - trying an advance from Alexandria, after previously capturing the Aboukir ports and Kafr ed-Dauar, he bemused the enemy in front of Alexandria, and then, deceiving everyone, including his own generals he, by an admirable series of combinations, in concert with the Navy, seized the Canal, and transferred his base to Ismailia. When there, instead of a rapid and showy dash into the heart of the country, which might have succeeded, but would have involved great risk, much loss of life, and would have won him only a first victory, to be followed by a prolonged campaign, he decided to wait until he had matured all his arrangements for one crushing blow, which should end the campaign,

History has to be consulted to determine whether Arabi was a pure-minded patriot labouring for the nationalisation of his country; an unscrupulous and ambitious mutineer aiming at taking the country over from the Khedive; or a mere tool of the Sultan of Turkey in his aim of restoring full Turkish power in Egypt. Whatever the truth of the matter, it cannot be denied that Arabi was a man of great determination, as shown by what he accomplished in his country in a very short time; his relatively rapid downfall was only brought about by the intensive effort of raising a major expeditionary force by the sole major power unwilling to allow the rise of a dictator likely to affect its interests."

We can well imagine Sergeant-Major Ash in Blackpool, looking back on this extraordinary expedition to Egypt, and his part in it. After the battle and after a pleasant six weeks in Cairo the battalion left that place on October 31 and embarked at Alexandria by half-battalions, which reached London two weeks later. He was going to be wearing medals now and there was to be a big parade in London for the victorious troops. What a wonderful day that must have been. How he must have wished, in that final weekend of his life, that his son's story of Egypt would be as good.

Back at Wellington Barracks, after his promotion in the field it would be back to drilling and guard duty. To the ordinary man, I suppose, being a colour-sergeant means the parade ground, drill and training. The drill manual would be his bible - he would know it thoroughly and, in time, instinctively. George Ash became a sergeant-major in 1894 when he transferred to the Lancashire Fusiliers.

A new issue of the Drill Manual was published in 1889. I chanced upon it when I was in Edinburgh Library researching the Scots Guards. The library staff extracted this little book from their archives. It was about the size of the palm of a large man's hand. Held together with string, the book almost fell apart as I opened its pages. The introduction was by none other than Lord Wolseley, who, having moved on from the 1882 campaign in Egypt and the attempt to rescue Gordon in Khartoum, was now a peer and the senior soldier in the land.

His introduction to the drill manual read:-

Horse Guards
War Office

1st January 1889

His Royal Highness The Commander-in-Chief has received the Queen's command to require of Officers a scrupulous adherence to the system of Drill and Manoeuvres now promulgated. The careful training of the soldier in ordinary times by those whose duty it will be to direct his fire and lead him in action has become of paramount importance.

These regulations are based on the principle of demanding great exactitude in the simplified movements still retained for Drill, while conceding the utmost latitude to all commanders, of however small a unit, in Manoeuvre. The first must be carried out literally, the second must be observed in the spirit more than the letter.

The very process by which the rank and file are gradually imbued with a feeling of confidence when called upon to act more or less upon their individual judgement, will create the discipline essential to success.

It is to the appreciation by General Officers Commanding of their vital points, and to their realising the altered conditions of modern warfare, that His Royal Highness looks for the efficient preparation of Infantry for the practical requirements of the battlefield.

By Command of His Royal Highness
The Commander-in-Chief

Wolseley, A. G.

Sergeant-Major Ash would have studied for hours the very manual I was reading. Its contents, under 'Marching' covered squad drill and company drill, then formations and movements of soldiers in battalion and brigade strength. Under 'Manoeuvre' it covered tactics as influenced by fire, advanced and rear guards, outposts, skirmishing, attack and defence and conduct of operations at night. All this, Sergeant-Major Ash would have been familiar with in Egypt; we can be certain that if Sergeant-Major Ash was familiar with this drill, then so would the infantrymen he trained.

The portrait of Private George Vivian Ash by Mark Adams, painted from the photograph in the Bury and District Soldier's Memorial Book 1914 - 15 edition published by the Bury Times.   (Courtesy of the Artist)

Chapter 7

Private George Vivian Ash 1884 - 1915

I can imagine George and Lizzie Ash boarding a train at Bolton Street Station in Bury bound for Blackpool on that final week-end of the Sergeant-Major's life. It was only a short walk from School Brow into Rock Street (now known as The Rock) past the Parish Church and then, pausing to buy the *Bury Times,* into the station. As they set off on their short journey what news would they share from the local paper? I doubt they would take much notice of the report from the Dardanelles. There was no special reason to be interested. George would know that the 1st Battalion, Lancashire Fusiliers was formed up as part of the 29th Division but still held in reserve in the Midlands, more likely to go to France than anywhere. But if they had taken any interest they would have read a short report in the 6th March edition on the February naval attack on the Dardanelles couched in unremarkable terms:-

"The attack on the Dardanelles has been resumed... British battleships did good work attacking the forts within the Straits. The French have begun an attack on the Bulair fortifications ... As before, the main British force employed itself in the Straits against the forts protecting the Narrows, where the channel is just over a mile in width, with operations here forming the most difficult part of the task of the Allied Fleet. Outside the Straits two light cruisers, the Dublin and the Sapphire, were busy and inflicted loss on the enemy. The French ships pursued their task in the Gulf of Xeros - there they harassed the Turks in the Bulair lines, and destroyed the bridge at Katack, through which passes the only road to the Gallipoli Peninsula. Unofficial messages report substantial progress against the interior forts."

Although the above report was in fact of events which were to be central to the ultimate defeat at Gallipoli, George and Lizzie would have been more interested in the piece about "The Battle of the Suez Canal", George because of his service in Egypt 33 years earlier, and both of them because their son was serving there. The *Bury Times* published two letters from local servicemen with the 42nd East Lancashire (Territorial) Division of which Private George Vivian Ash's battalion was part.

Corporal Hilton writes to his wife in Radcliffe (near Bury):-

---

THE BATTLE OF THE SUEZ CANAL

A RADCLIFFE CORPORAL'S ACCOUNT.

"We have been in action. So far as I am aware, only the Royal Engineers and the 1st and 2nd sections of the Bolton Artillery, out of the whole division, have had that honour. The casualties were, I am pleased to say, very small, and the Territorials acquitted themselves well. The Indians are splendid fighters. The alarm went about 4 a.m. on the 3rd (March 1915). We had been expecting it for several nights, so it did not cause much surprise. We fell in and marched off, laughing and joking. Little did we know that the enemy were so near on the opposite bank of the canal. Several of the sharpshooters had crept right to the edge of the water in the darkness."

The second account goes further:-

"The Turks tried to get across the canal at several places, but we drove them back, and captured over a thousand prisoners. They were a motley crowd, I can tell you. Some were without shoes, and had very little clothing. We had 200 of them at Ismailia (where Sergeant-Major Ash had been in 1882). We also took 24 pontoons, as well as thousands of rounds of ammunition, rifles and bayonets. Our Jack Tars and the French did some splendid work, as also the Bolton and Blackburn artillery. You should have seen those Turks scatter. They have cleared off back. Before I left Ismalia they had retired 40 miles. We don't know if they intend coming back but if they do they will get a bigger surprise next time. There are plenty of shells knocking about on the desert."

George Ash would have been alert to the reference to Ismailia. This is where his ship, the *Orient* docked with the Scots Guards in August 1882 on their way to the Battle of Tel El-Kebir and the occupation of Cairo. The disparaging reference to the Turks is interesting. This poor view of their fighting qualities was widely held and pervaded all the way up in the Army and in political circles as well. It illustrates very well the impact of leadership on the fighting effectiveness of an army. At Gallipoli the Turks were well led and, in defending their homeland, very brave. They were to be fatally under-estimated. After the first awful day of the attack on Gallipoli the army, which was expecting an easy occupation of the high ground, were numbed by the reality. But their son was in Egypt and while the Turks posed no serious threat to the army there, George and Lizzie would have had no fears for their son.

Another soldier wrote home wanting a bit more action than he was seeing.
He wrote:-

LETTER FROM EGYPT

"Though the last six months have been rather crowded ones, I have not forgotten my Radcliffe friends, and am looking to the day when I shall see you all
again. As far as active service is concerned, I have not realised my hopes, as to
us has fallen the monotonous duty of garrisoning Khartoum, which is just as
peaceful as Radcliffe, even if it is a little warmer. The rest of the division in
Egypt may see some fighting; in fact, there has been some 'scrapping' on the
canal already, but I am afraid that we shall be left out of the fun. We had a hope
that we should be relieved in February, but that has been extinguished with the
war with Turkey, and we seem to be doomed to remain here some time. Life
here is not so very exciting - a good deal of work without the excitement of war,
and, as far as one can see, not much prospect. We are up at 5:30 each morning,
and get our work done by mid-day, the heat is too great to do much after
noon ..."

We can expect George Ash to have given a wry smile when reading about the
heat; as we have seen, he did not like it himself when he was in Egypt.

It was now six months since they had said goodbye to George Vivian, who
had lost no time, on the outbreak of war on 4th August 1914, in rejoining his
Territorial battalion, the 5th, soon to be renamed the 1st/5th, to make way for
sequentially numbered new territorial battalions, the 2nd/5th and the 3rd/5th,
all comprising Bury men.

Recruiting had been brisk. The *Bury Times* had recalled, on the day after war
broke out, the legendary past of the Lancashire Fusiliers by publishing the
following:-

MINDEN DAY

Saturday was the anniversary of the battle of Minden, fought August 1st, 1759,
between the English, Hessians, and Hanoverians and the French. The
Lancashire Fusiliers, then the 20th Foot, played a prominent part. They had to
pass through a garden of roses, and many of the soldiers bedecked themselves
with the flowers. On Saturday, in commemoration of the anniversary,
Lancashire Fusiliers quartered at the depot, Wellington Barracks, Bury, wore
red roses in their caps.

The Minden 'Yell' was legendary. Sergeant-Major Ash would have been imbued with its spirit. The French commander, Contades, who lost the battle of Minden, remarked bitterly:

"I never thought to see a single line of infantry break through three lines of cavalry ranked in order of battle, and to tumble them to ruin".

The commander of the Allied troops, Prince Ferdinand, visiting the battle-field (in Germany) 38 years later, said: *"It was here the conflict was most obstinate, and it was here that the British infantry gained immortal glory".* Minden Day is cele-brated still today, nearly 250 years later: it seems the Prince was right! At a recruitment meeting in Bury on 9 December 1914, Admiral Lord Charles Beresford MP said:-

"I know the Lancashire Fusiliers. When their ammunition is expended they will use their bayonets and when their bayonets are broken they will use their fists".

The Lancashire Fusiliers were a crack regiment: George and his son were serving with it. Lizzie Ash would have been proud of them both and my grand-mother too. As the last week-end of the Sergeant-Major's life and the last happy week-end of Lizzie Ash's life were spent peacefully in Blackpool, there was time to reflect on the six months since they had seen their son and his life in Egypt. Within a few weeks of him joining up after war broke out he had left for Egypt. How dramatically life had changed! How tragic it was to become!

On 5 September 1914 the *Bury Times* had reported that the 5th Battalion had been filled up to its full establishment and that excess supplies of recruits had enlisted into the 6th (Rochdale) and 7th (Salford) Battalions. In due course, the 8th Battalion (Salford) was formed to make the Lancashire Fusiliers Territorial Brigade of the 42nd East Lancashire Territorial Division. The new battalion had been sent in August to a camp at Turton near Bury where exercising and training took place. The men were invited to waive their "Home Defence Only" status and all bar a handful duly did. Thus, they made themselves available for over-seas service: who knows how many believed what they were told - that they would go to some colonial station with a healthy climate! In any event specula-tion was rife about where the Division would actually go. No one could guess it was doomed to end up in Gallipoli.

There was no doubt Sergeant-Major George Ash would stay at home. At his age and experience his job would be to train recruits. I have not been able to determine exactly when he re-joined the Army but the evidence suggests it was October 1914. Whether it was spontaneous or in response to specific requests for older former NCO's to re-join I don't know. On 5 September the *Bury Times* reports the Mayor's recruitment drive with handbills having been put out all over the town. In these it was stated, so far as older former NCO's were concerned, that recruits up to the age of 50 were required. George Ash was already 56: it is quite easy to understand how, for a man of his reputation, and the general mood of volunteering, the age limit was waived. Indeed, the *Bury Times* trumpeted:-

THE VOLUNTEERS OF BURY

HISTORICAL SKETCH

At the present time the people of Bury are almost enthusiastically military. They are proud of the association of the Lancashire Fusiliers with their town, and prouder still of the possession of a Volunteer Battalion of which all inspecting officers, even the sternest, have a good word to say. Their military instincts are not a thing of yesterday, but are bred in the bones. From the beginning of their national history Englishmen have been liable to sudden calls telling of danger to the State or the home.

No doubt all that was going on, what with both her husband and her son in the famous regiment, swept Lizzie Ash along. Not many had any idea what was to come. England hadn't been at war in Europe since Waterloo almost 100 years earlier. Warfare had changed, unrecognisably. The world was to change, unrecognisably. This was to be no four and a half month expedition that her husband had joined in 1882 with its easy, albeit well earned, victory. This was the start of a period of unmitigated grief for Lizzie Ash and her daughters. But for now it was time to say goodbye to Private George Vivian Ash - she would not see him again. The *Bury Times* reported on the Brigade leaving Bury on 9/10 September 1914:-

THE TURTON CAMP

The entraining of the Bury Battalion of Lancashire Fusiliers and the other battalions which had been encamped at Turton took place at stations in the vicinity. The roads which led on to the stations ... were quite impassable, and one could not get within 200 or 300 yards ... The Lancashire Fusiliers all looked fit and well, the excellent effects of the training in such healthy surroundings being reflected in their bronzed faces. The Bolton and Blackburn brigades of artillery marched to Bolton, and their passage ... furnished an occasion for much excitement. The men were heartily greeted by the crowds. The steep declines and the stiff inclines which are to be found on the road from Turton occasionally proved a stumbling block to many of the horses owing to the slightly greasy surface, but the treacherous parts were all safely negotiated. Many of the trains conveying men and horses from the Turton camp passed through Knowsley Street Station, Bury.

SPECIAL TRAINS UTILISED

About forty special trains were required for the conveyance of the East Lancashire Division ... The personnel included 588 officers and 18,000 men. There were also 5,600 horses, 36, 15-pounder guns, 12 howitzers, 24 machine guns, 239 carts, about 400 wagons and tons of baggage.

    The last unit did not leave camp until nearly midnight on Wednesday. The only troops left behind are those who have elected to confine their duties to home defence...

None of the Ash family papers have come into my hands - this was, as already noted, a huge void. No doubt Private Ash wrote home, but what he said, what he thought is unknown. I can be pretty sure however, that the family would have read the numerous letters that other members of the 1st/5th Battalion wrote home and which were published in the *Bury Times*.

One letter describes the journey, the food and the conditions in barracks in Cairo:

"THE SIGHT OF A LIFETIME"

———

"Sorry to keep you waiting so long for word, but I could not get any writing material on board, only one sheet of paper, which I sent home from Gibralter. They soon got us down to Southampton, and on the way we passed Sutton's Seed Gardens (demolished in the late 1960's), and we also saw the flying machines at Brooklands (this was the Vickers factory and airfield, now redeveloped) ... We stayed in the bay at Gibralter a few hours, and it was a splendid sight. The natives put off in small boats, selling fruit and tobacco... The first three days on board we could hardly eat anything, through being sick, but afterwards we did not get enough. Each man received one loaf for his breakfast and tea each day ... but I had to spend my pay on extra food. It is considered an offense to sell food to troops on board, but we used to go to the bakers at night ... and they charged very high prices. In the canteen at first it was 2d for Woodbines, then 1d, then 4d, and 9d for Gold Flake; 3d for a small piece of cake.
A great many of our men preferred sleeping on deck to going below in a hammock, but we had to get up soon to allow them to swill the decks ... After fifteen days we landed at Alexandria, and it was the sight of a lifetime ... We were served out with helmets there, and then we entrained for Cairo ... (The barracks are) built entirely of stone and a kind of concrete only the doors and window frames being wood ... we can see two of the great pyramids ... ten miles away. While on the ship the officers lectured us a great deal on the importance of cleanliness, and on board we had a canvas bath; but here we have shower baths and can use them when we like. You cannot be too clean, as the flies and insects are a perfect pest, and there is so much sand flying about. I have not been out to Cairo, and I have no drill suit yet, but they say it is a gay place, full of amusements. Frank Fitton is all right now he has got the printing shop, with extra pay. One of the 3rd Dragoons who has now gone to the front, told me that we can see some of the finest carvings and sculpture in the native churches, so I shall be having a good look round. Hoping work is good, and you are doing full time*.
Remember me to all at the shop."

---

* This is a reminder that unemployment or short time working was endemic in the cotton industry in Lancashire. This indeed is the reason the XXth Regiment of Foot came to Bury in the first place before changing its name to the Lancashire Fusiliers.

Another correspondent, Private Joe Smethurst, of Bury, writes to his parents:-

---

SCENES IN CAIRO

———

"We arrived at Alexandria 24 September, and ... left by train for Abbassia ... something like the size of Bury, a distance of about 120 miles and two miles from Cairo. The trains are rather dangerous, because where each carriage is coupled up it is open, and if one is not careful when going into another carriage he may very easily fall out, and I regret to state that one of our sergeants fell out and was killed instantly ...

With regard to our sea voyage, ... was glad when we got to Alexandria. Following my week at Turton, sleeping on oil sheets, we had a fortnight on board ship, sleeping in the bottom on a hard floor ... Now we are in barracks we have had the first two nights in the same fashion - sleeping on the floor ...

For breakfast we got dry bread and tea; for dinner a choice roast but no vegetables; for tea, dry bread and such meat as was left over from dinner. However, I have no doubt matters will improve when we get more settled. This is soldiering proper. What do you say - shall I not value my home when I get back? The other night we took a car for Cairo, and spent a lively two hours in that city. Cairo appears to me to be something like the size of Manchester, and possesses some very fine buildings. But oh! What sights we met with! The people are mostly coloured, with an odd Frenchman here and there. They came rushing to meet us, with all kinds of fancy articles, including such things as silks, rings, post-cards, beads, watches, and chains, and heaps of other things ... Mother and Florrie would feel rather strange walking down Rock Street surrounded by coloured men and women, shaking their fists and pulling all kinds of funny faces. But they are quite harmless if left alone, and I think it is more their fun than anything else, as they laugh heartily at every white man as he walks down the street. Still, we have been warned to keep in the main street ...

It is something like eight degrees hotter now than the hottest summer's day in England, but the winter is now coming on so it must be almost unbearable in summer. The only thing one need seriously grumble about are the flies; while I am writing this I have to keep knocking them off my hands. All our battalion seem in the best of health and spirits, and as long as everything is kept clean and orderly I do not see that we need take much harm."

The reference to flies reminds us that they were a huge curse on the men in Gallipoli.

In the first few weeks of her widowhood Lizzie Ash would not have had much cause to fear for her son. In its 10th April issue, the *Bury Times* published another letter from Egypt:-

---

HOTTER THAN SOUTHPORT

"The weather is becoming hotter here every day. I am sure it must be above 100° F here at mid-day. The other day we had a march to the desert starting at 8:30 a.m. and finishing at 2:30 p.m. The work we are doing in this awfully hot climate is no child's play. I do not know what it will be like in summer. I saw a letter in your February issue (which found its way to Egypt from Bury) stating that this place is superior to Southport. Anyway, let me have Southport. There are no amusements here as at Southport. We have completely routed the Turks, a battery of Territorials Artillery also..."

The March naval bombardment in the Dardanalles was reported in the *Bury Times* as if it were a bit of sport:-

---

"The (HMS) Queen Elizabeth (a brand new battleship fresh from the builder's yard)... made good practice at 21,000 yards range. The Queen Elizabeth and other battleships ... bombarded the forts on the European side of the Dardanelles narrows from across the Gallipoli peninsula."

There was no hint of a land war and no speculation of such. But before April was out, this was to change. In the meanwhile, Lizzie Ash was grieving the loss of her husband.

The first reference to the Dardanelles in the *Bury Times*, so far as the Lancashire Fusiliers were concerned, is in a letter home published on 24 April, just one day prior to the invasion at dawn on the 25th. Writing to his local Councillor, Private J. Chadwick, of 5th Battalion Lancashire Fusiliers writes:

TOTTINGTON LADS IN EGYPT

"I have been asked by several of the Tottington lads to thank you for the kind words you sent to the newspapers concerning the welfare of the Tottington lads. I think it was very well constructed, and I might say that all the lads were well pleased with it. All the boys are looking as well as can be expected, but we are all fed up with this monotonous life. I think it won't be long before we move, and probably Constantinople (! !) will be our destination. Of course I am only surmising, but I cannot see going elsewhere. As you are aware, it is not our fault that we are not in action. We have asked to go either to
Continued on next page ....

---

the Dardanelles (! !) or to France, but we are told that our services here are very valuable. They tell us that the Protectorate of Egypt is very important. When one realises
that three parts of the exports of this country are cotton, I think it is worth looking after;
and when it is obvious that Lancashire lads should look after their own interests. No
doubt you are aware that we are stationed at -------------- about ------* miles from the
capital, Cairo. We had four months here when we first landed but we went to
Alexandria. This is by the sea, and it is a large commercial or business place. It is
termed the Liverpool of Egypt. We spent two months at Alexandria, and I was
astounded at the amount of cotton turned out. The bay is full of German ships. I think
there will be about twenty-five. Our job was guarding the prisoners from these ships.
The weather has been about 80 degrees, just passable; but we are told that next month
(April) we get it about 105 degrees, so you must expect us looking like the Egyptians
when we get home - that is if we don't move. I will write you again shortly, and
forward you some postcards of the place. Again thanking you on behalf of the lads
and myself."

It is an extraordinary breach of security to allow surmise about
Constantinople - it was published in Bury the day before the attack on Gallipoli -
being the probable destination, while the censor contented himself with striking
out the name of the camp in Egypt and its distance from the capital, which were
details of no strategic importance. In the same issue there was a tub-thumping
compliment about the fighting qualities of the 42nd East Lancashire Territorial
Division. The *Bury Times* reported:-

PRAISE FOR TERRITORIALS

'The General Officer Commanding Mediteranean Force having been accorded the privilege of reviewing the East Lancashire Division, wishes to congratulate the General
Officer Commanding the troops in Egypt, as well as Major-General Douglas, on the turn
out and soldierly bearing of that Force. During the past seven months some hundreds
of thousands of Territorials have passed under Sir Ian Hamilton's command, and he was
able to observe to-day that the East Lancashire Division have made full use of the
advantages which fine weather and the absence of billeting have given them over their
comrades now bearing arms, whether at home or on the Continent of Europe. Ever
since the siege of Ladysmith, General Sir Ian Hamilton has interested himself specially
in the military output of Manchester, and it is a real pleasure to him now to be able to
bear witness to the fact that this great city is being so finely represented in the East."

---

* Obliterated by the censor. It seems bizarre that he should be fussed about where the 42nd Division was bar-
racked but should allow open speculation about the Dardanelles and Constantinople.

The *Bury Times* also reported a letter from Private McCrakan who said:-

> "We are looking smart in every little detail, and are hoping the time will not be far distant when we can share our worth. We get your valuable paper every fortnight and I for one can tell you am always eager to learn local news."

This is the sort of stuff in which a mother takes pride. In the same (24 April) edition of the paper Lizzie Ash may have been alarmed by:-

> "With regard to the Dardanelles, an English correspondent wired that he had received a message stating that ... the allied fleet was bombarding places on the Gallipoli Isthmus, where the Turks had for some considerable time been working on fortifications. A report from Athens says that great activity was noted among the British at Lemnos, troops and transports arriving daily from Alexandria. A report issued from Constantinople states that two ironclads on Tuesday fired unsuccessfully at long range over one hundred shells upon the batteries in the Dardanelles.
>
>   General Sir Ian Hamilton has taken command of the Ango-French army employed against Turkey."

If a report like that was circulating in Bury on the eve of the biggest amphibious operation ever undertaken against modern weaponry, we can be sure that the Turks and their German masters were equally aware that attack was imminent. As we shall see, there was to be neither strategical nor tactical surprise when the attack went in.

News of the attack on Gallipoli at dawn on 25 April 1915 broke on Wednesday 28 April 1915 when the *Bury Times* reported:-

> "The landing of British troops in considerable forces at various points of the Gallipoli Peninsula, and the resumption of the general attack on the Dardanelles by the Allied Fleet indicate that the operations for forcing the Straight and reaching Constantinople have begun again on a formidable scale, with the naval and military forces on this occasion combined to achieve the great object of the expedition. The landing of the troops took place before sunrise on Sunday, under cover of the Fleet, and despite the serious opposition of the enemy, who was strongly entrenched, proved completely successful. The War Office state that the landing of the army and the advance continue."

There was no mention yet of the 1st Battalion being involved in the landings. With the blinkers now in place the *Bury Times* reported on 1st May:-

> "News from the Dardanelles is good. The British troops who landed on Sunday have made sure of their ground. They hold securely the sea end of the Gallipoli peninsula, occupying some five square miles of ground, which will provide an excellent base for the advance upon the European shore of the Straits. From the Gulf of Saros coast also excellent progress has been made. One landing force has advanced to Saribair, some miles from the sea, and after defeating heavy Turkish attacks, is advancing. Saribair is within six miles of the Dardanelles passage above the Narrows. An unofficial report says that the Allies have taken some thousands of prisoners, including many German officers."

With official sources being the only ones available, the *Bury Times* was obliged to trumpet:-

> "A gratifying report of the Allies' progress in the Dardanelles, in the form of a review of the operations from the first landing on Sunday morning up to Thursday evening, was issued on Friday night by the War Office and the Admiralty. The effect of it is that three military forces are now fairly established on Turkish territory. They had to overcome a desperate resistance, but are now steadily advancing. The Australians and New Zealanders had the hottest fighting. The Allied Fleet, having covered the landing operations, has now turned its attention to the forts. Our casualties are reported to be heavy. The King has congratulated all ranks on their splendid achievement. A correspondent at Athens telegraphed on Monday: 'Four large transports of Germans have been sent as reinforcements to the Dardanelles. A big panic reigns in Constantinople.' "

But, as it happened, things had gone badly wrong. The landings had taken place, certainly, but three unpalatable truths now haunted Hamilton, the Commander-in-Chief. His troops had not captured the high ground: he had suffered very heavy casualties and the Turks were fighting for their lives with no fear of death. On the very day that the *Bury Times* reported that: *"A big panic reigns in Constantinople"*, Hamilton, casting around for reinforcements to replace his losses, fell on the 42nd East Lancashire Division who left their barracks and entrained for Alexandria on 1 May, seven days after the attack started. They left Alexandria at 6:20 a.m. on the 3rd arriving off the Cape Helles in the afternoon of the 5th. The next day the 1st/5th Battalion disembarked onto the Lancashire Landing beach, which their own 1st Battalion had won so gloriously 11 days earlier. But none of this was known in Bury. The first knowledge that the Ash family had that the 42nd East Lancashire Division had left Egypt and was in combat in Gallipoli was by a reference to the Territorials when the *Bury Times* reported on 22nd May:-

"The progress of the Allies in the Dardanelles continues. An official report from General Sir Ian Hamilton, issued on Wednesday, states that every day sees improvements in the Anglo-French position. (He was always optimistic in nature). In the first battle our army was drawn up in the following order:- On the extreme left the 87th Brigade held the great donga* and the trenches on the hills beyond. The line was prolonged to the right by the 88th Brigade, and then on to the Krithia road by part of the Naval Division. On the other side of the road was another Brigade of the same Division. Behind the line the Indian Brigade, the Australians, and New Zealanders stood in reserve, and **behind them the newly-arrived Territorial Division** (author's emphasis). On the right the French stood, with the blue-coated Senegalese in their front line, ... the Foreign Legion in reserve. **Since then the Lancashire Territorials have played a prominent part** (author's emphasis), especially in the advance made on the nights of the 16th and 17th inst. The Turks are reported to have suffered very heavy losses."

By the time Lizzie Ash read this, her son had already been in action; suddenly he was involved in something that was a good deal more than a raid on the Suez Canal. He would be reported killed well before the enormity of it all would be realised. The heavy losses of the Turks are reported quickly but not those of the Allies. The report of 22 May continues:-

"Later, but unofficial, telegrams from Athens say the fighting in the Gallipoli Peninsula continues fiercely. ... the Allies delivered heavy attacks and captured Turkish positions. It is stated that the Kilid Bahr forts have been silenced and the enemy's main positions are in danger. Good progress would seem to have been made towards the forcing of the Narrows (this was false). When the troops reach Kilid Bahr (which they never did) they will have taken a great stride towards Constantinople. They will command the Narrows. Beyond the Narrows the Turkish defences are less formidable. The Straits widen, and the obstacles before a fleet desiring to enter the Sea of Marmora present fewer difficulties."

All that was being reported here was what Hamilton hoped to do, not what he had done. The cost of failure was becoming very heavy. The first news in the *Bury Times* alerting their readers to the fact that something awful had happened was on 26 May 1915. One month after the attack commenced, the chilling report reads:-

- see next page.

---

*   A steep-sided gully created by soil erosion.

CHAPLAIN'S STORY OF LANCASHIRE FUSILIERS HEROISM

A thrilling story of the heroism of the Lancashire Fusiliers has been written by the Rev. Harry Foster, formerly a Goole curate, and now chaplain to the 2nd Naval Brigade in the Dardanelles. Describing the landing, he says: "Those who went first had an awful time, especially the Dublin and Lancashire Fusiliers. In regiments the colonels were killed, the adjutants, and practically all the officers. On landing I found hundreds of wounded and dying. Most of them were the Lancashire Fusiliers, and to them belongs the honour of the day. They stormed up the stiff cliff with bayonets fixed, in face of a galling fire of rifles and maxims, but they carried the position and made it possible for us to land. They have won themselves everlasting renown. At night we buried the dead in the dark and with the aid of torches - 95 men in one grave and five in another, which had been dug by Turkish prisoners."

Imagine Lizzie Ash reading this. At first rushed reading she could scarcely have taken it in. Reading it again she would have gasped: "hundreds of wounded and dying": "Lancashire Fusiliers": "Oh my God; my son", she might have exclaimed, for there is nothing in the report to say that it was the 1st Battalion that had been mauled. But she would have been reassured for the safety of her son later, because on the same day the *Bury Guardian* published this encouraging piece:-

"On the eve of the departure of the East Lancashire Division for the Dardanelles, Sir John Maxwell sent a telegram to General Douglas, the general officer commanding the East Lancashire Division:

"When you have the opportunity will you let the East Lancashire Division know that during the time they have been under my command I have been filled with admiration of their conduct, keenness, capacity for hard work, cheerfulness and soldier-like spirit. Now they are going on hard active service I am sure they will fight gallantly and uphold the great traditions of Lancashire and the Empire, and prove if proof be needed, that the trained Territorial soldier is second to none."

It was a bit late for this sort of stuff: the cat was out of the bag - Lancashire Fusiliers were dying, but at least Lizzie would know that Vivian was not involved in the early ruinous invasion.

During May, official news of casualties started to arrive in Lancashire. No official word was given of the extent of the carnage until very much later. But the press got wind of the fact that something bad had happened to the Territorials and notices like that shown on the next page, from the *Bury Guardian,* began to appear and were repeated throughout the summer.

The Lancashire Fusiliers

———

Local Rank and File Casualties

———

Relatives and friends of those members of the 5th Battalion the Lancashire Fusiliers (Territorials) who have been engaged in the fighting in the Eastern area, and have been killed or wounded, are requested to notify the receipt of such news if communicated to them from official sources, at the Guardian offices as early as possible.

Thus, a conspiracy between the press and the bereaved families grew up - a conspiracy designed to outwit the official cover-up of the extent of the catastrophe. From May onwards the *Bury Times* had, on its front page of every issue, a new batch of photos with short biographic notes of *"Local Heroes who have given their lives for their Country"*.

No official word of the scale of the losses was to emerge until it had all been worked out from the number of grieving families. Colonel Hickey, author of a fine book on the subject,* tells a colourful story of how one Lancashire family heard of the facts in a way that defeated the censor: *"I can't mention casualties"* wrote a correspondent *"but they were: officers, the last numeral in the year we were married. Men about four fifths of my Wigan telephone number,"* In this roundabout way, says Hickey, and weeks before the official figures were released, the families of the Territorials were given the first dark hints of the tragedy in which their men were involved. When the scale, the enormity, of the losses dawned on the *Bury Times* they began a task which, started as a huge labour but which, in the final analysis, became Herculean in its scale. The *Bury Times* commenced the compilation of Bury and District Soldiers' Memorial Book, which ultimately was published in three volumes. Well might I have been disappointed, in my naivety, that the town war memorial had no names on it. How can a town cope with such losses ? How can such losses be memorialised ? The Territorial battalions, all Bury men in the 1st/5th, the 2nd/5th and the 3rd/5th Battalions lost 1,662 officers and men from a town with a population of around 50,000. The losses started with Gallipoli, but later they were to include the Western Front. To start the process of creating a record of the deaths, the *Bury Times* started advertising for help.

---

*   *Gallipoli* page 213.

Bury's Roll of Honour

Names Wanted

With regard to the official roll of honour which is being compiled in Bury, we are asked to call the attention of employers and others who have had men in their service who have enlisted in the army or navy to assist in the work by forwarding the names of such men to the Town Clerk as early as possible.

Later, with the help of the local authority, Bury Corporation, their huge task having been completed for the years 1914 and 1915, the *Bury Times* advertised their great work.

NOW READY !

THE FIRST PART OF THE

**BURY & DISTRICT
SAILORS AND SOLDIERS'
MEMORIAL BOOK,**

CONTAINING

OVER 530 PORTRAITS
and brief particulars of men to
the number of over 600 from Bury
and District who laid down their
lives for their Country in the Great War.

**in this section only those who fell
in 1914 - 15 are included**

SEPARATE SECTIONS FOR
SUCCEEDING YEARS TO FOLLOW.

Price 2/6 ; by Post 2/8.

MAY BE OBTAINED FROM

THE "TIMES" OFFICE

BURY

OR THROUGH ANY NEWSAGENT

It wasn't until June that news of the deaths of Bury men from the 1st/5th Battalion started appearing in the *Bury Times**. On 2 June they reported that:-

> " ... official intimation was received on Friday by Mrs. Haslam that her husband, Private Ernest Haslam, of the 1st/5th Lancashire Fusiliers, had been killed in action in the Dardanelles. He had been a member of the 1st V.B.L.F. (Sergeant-Major Ash's Battalion) for 14 years, and on the outbreak of the war he enlisted in the Territorials, and went with them to Egypt."

It was now getting very close to home. Private Haslam's mother had been at the funeral of the Sergeant-Major in March. Having been in the 1st Volunteer battalion for fourteen years, to say he would have known both George and Vivian Ash, who was two years younger, very well, would be an understatement.

On 5 June the official report was still sanguine:-

> "Hard hand-to-hand fighting in the Dardanelles has cost the Turks very many casualties. The Allies have beaten off violent attacks and hold all their positions. Turkish prisoners report that the Ottoman losses in Gallipoli have been terribly heavy, totalling a fortnight ago 40,000 killed and wounded. A British submarine in the Sea of Marmora on Wednesday torpedoed a large German transport in Panderma Bay. At the head of the bay is a military base for the Asiatic troops on their way to the Dardanelles. The Vice Admiral at the Dardanelles, in reporting the affair, speaks of the vessel as 'one of the British submarines at present operating' within the Straits. Only a day or two earlier a message from Athens reported that two Turkish transports had been sunk somewhere between Constantinople and Gallipoli".

Bury people could see through this: with reports of casualties and deaths coming in daily, there was no assuaging their sorrow. On 5 June, by which time the news of the death of Vivian Ash's friend Ernest Haslam was already known, the *Bury Times* reported:-

> Writing under the date 10 May, Private Hatch of the Signaller's Section of the 1st/5th now operating in the Dardanelles says in a letter received by his parents this week:-
>
> 'I am writing you once more, but under difficult conditions. We disembarked last Wednesday (6 May) and were in action on Thursday. Our casualties were pretty heavy. I dare not tell you any more at present. (Ominous !) I am in the pink and still in one piece.'

---

* The regulars in the 1st Battalion, whose losses at Lancashire Landing were so great, were not particularly from Bury. The Territorial battalions were all local men.

On the same day, was published accompanying portraits of two Tennant brothers, both of whom were serving with the 1st/5th.

According to a letter received by their mother, Mrs Tennant, dated May 10th, Harry Tennant was killed in action on Friday, May 7th. The letter says:-

'My Dear Mother, - I suppose you will have received official advice of our dear Harry's death long before you get this letter. I was just near Harry at the time, and I am sure it will be some consolation to you to know that his death was instantaneous and painless. He fell with his face to the enemy, and I am sure no man could wish for a more glorious death. I am sure, dear mother, that you and I can quite understand each other's feelings, and we must pray to God to give us strength to bear the great loss which we have sustained. I cannot give you any names of places, but I will do so as soon as permissible.'

More reassuringly, in the same issue, appeared the following letter from Herbert Walmsley of the 1st/5th Lancashire Fusiliers to his parents:-

BURY TERRIERS IN THE DARDANELLES
TOBACCO & CIGARETTES WANTED

'By the time you get this you will probably have heard that we have been in action. Well, so we have, and I am very glad to be able to tell you that I am still alive and in the best of health. Some of my friends were hit, one fatally. You will send me tobacco and cigarettes every week, please. Give my respects to all friends. We are living in dug-outs. We have been in the trenches. Very exciting, I assure you.'

This man survived Gallipoli, but died on the Western Front in July 1918: this letter would have given some comfort, but the next to be published, from Percy Round, also to his parents, would set a mother worrying:

UNDER SHELL FIRE

'We landed here last Wednesday night, in navy boats. It was an all night job. We were frozen with cold, sleeping on the sea shore. We could hear the fierce battle raging a few miles away. The naval guns were firing all night. We marched inland early on Thursday and bivouacked near the firing line in holes and trenches. There was plenty of shrapnel bursting all around. One man was hit within a few yards of me. Had many narrow escapes from being riddled. There were stray bullets flying all over the place long before we reached the firing line. After walking along trenches a mile or two a party of us made a dash and reached the top of a ravine or gully. Before we had been there many minutes a maxim gun began firing at us. We stayed there some time. It

SIMPLY RAINED BULLETS.

(continued on next page)

At last we managed to crawl back to the trenches, and afterwards tried to get away, but the maxim gun spotted us; and the same thing happened again. After falling back a second time we were shelled with shrapnel, but finally managed to get away, returning to the base at night fagged out, having been relieved by another Battalion. It was a marvel how the lot of us escaped being killed. One or two were killed and wounded near me, but I came through without being hit. The place was full of machine guns and snipers, and we could not find where they were hidden. We are living in holes (dug-outs) to protect us from shells; and for food we have biscuits and bully beef. No dainties here. We have been shelled several times. One shell dropped within fifty yards of us, but luckily did not explode. A few of our Battalion have been killed; and plenty wounded, mostly slight wounds on arm or leg. We are under shellfire as I write this. I am in good health and all right, but don't know how I shall go on.'

After pointing out that he has not received any letters or papers since leaving Alexandria he jocularly remarks that: *'active service is all right but for the shells and other things flying about. We don't know where they are going to hit'* he adds, *'but always hope for the best"*. In another letter he says they hear awful tales about the treatment of men captured by the Turks, so they did not intend to be captured so long as they had ammunition or a bayonet at the end of a rifle - Gallipoli and the bayonet go hand in hand.

Private Gilbert V. Buxton (son of Mr. R. W. Buxton, the Borough Treasurer), who was with the 1st/5th Battalion in the Dardanelles, wrote to his parents from the Firing Line on May 10th, saying:-

'Just a line, which I hope you will receive safely, to let you know that up to the present I am in good health and spirits. We had the first application of our training in an attack on Friday last. It was a terrible time for our men, but we stuck it bravely, and I think very creditably, in spite of the mowing down of a large number of our comrades. We scouts were out two or three hours before the battalion set out and had a pretty hot reception, but all of us, with the exception of our officer, came through untouched. .... I leave out details of the battle, and rely on being able to give them in person some time later. ... We are in 'dug-outs' within hearing of the rifle fire, and pretty comfortable, though we find it cold at night.'

This man, being the Borough Treasurer, would have known Vivian Ash from business, as well as being in the same battalion - he died two days later on 6 June.

Private George Vivian Ash died in the 3rd Battle of Krithia on 4th June 1915. His wife and mother knew on 3rd July. In the Wednesday, 7th July 1915 issue of the *Bury Times* there were no less than 28 such heroes whose death was announced. Private Ash's picture appeared, on account of the alphabet, in the top left hand slot. During the period when I was researching the circumstances of

Vivian's death being reported I was in touch with a remarkable man, a member of the Gallipoli Association, who has accumulated a huge stock of knowledge on the casualties in Gallipoli. His name is Pat Gareipy. When I e-mailed him, somewhat routinely to enquire if he new anything of my man, who was when all is said and done, just one of 44,000 killed in the campaign, I have to admit I had no elevated expectations. His reply, which came in an instant, was so dramatic that I reproduce it below in full. That part of the text that was new information to me is underlined and emboldened:-

---

ASH, Private George Vivian
No. 2007 1/5th Battalion (T.F.) The Lancashire Fusiliers
Born in Chelsea, London, and enlisted in Bury, Lancashire, the eldest son of the late Sergeant Major George Ash of the 1st Volunteer battalion The Lancashire Fusiliers (later of the 2/5th Battalion). Husband of Bessie Ash of 76, Heywood Street, Bury **(Later of 9 Wilson Street, Bury).** Father of **Frederick Marsh Ash (born February 22, 1914).** He was educated at the Bury Parish Church School and was employed as chief clerk for the Bury Tramways Corporation from **1906** until the outbreak of war. For several years he had been a member of the 1st V.B. The Lancashire Fusiliers, eventually taking his discharge. In August 1914 he re-enlisted in Bury and on June 4, 1915, he was killed in action at the Third Battle of Krithia, aged 30 years. **Mrs. Ash was notified of her husband's death on Saturday, July 3, 1915. A memorial service was held for Private Ash on Tuesday night, July 6, 1915, at St. Thomas' Church in Bury and was officiated by the Rev. F.W. Rideal. Another was held in the Bury Parish Church at 7 p.m. on Wednesday, July 7, 1915, and was officiated by the Rev. J.C. Hill.** Name commemorated on the Helles memorial. Photo, death notice, report and report of his Memorial service in *The Bury Times* of July 7, 1915; report of his memorial service in the issue of July 10, 1915. **Mrs. Ash received her husband's separation allowance until January 2, 1916, and she began receiving a pension of 15 shillings per week the following day (January 3). Their son received a pension until he reached the age of 16.**

For your story, keep in mind that the 1st/5th landed at Gallipoli wearing leather cavalry bandoleers and belt pouches instead of P08 webbing, due to a shortage of the latter.

If I can be of any further help, please feel free to ask.
Regards, Pat.

To have such facts at your finger tip for what was for Pat Gareipy a randomly selected soldier is truly stunning. The only missing details, one might jest, are what time of day the postman arrived with the telegram and what he'd had for breakfast! But one detail was stunning: Vivian Ash had a son, Fred, who was only 15 months old when his father died. He had been given the name "Marsh", which was the maiden name of his grandmother from Dorset. Perhaps the existence of a baby explains why one of the aunts was missing at Sergeant-Major Ash's funeral - someone would have to look after Fred: but what became of the baby, of whom I have never heard mention?

I can scarcely imagine the family grief that was suffered: neither Bessie Ash nor Lizzie Ash (George Ash's widow) did I know, but my grandmother survived until 1965, forty years later. The loss of her brother could still bring a tear to her eyes when she spat The Dardanelles' name. I do not think it over indulgent of me to bring to this account a tearful story related by Geoffrey Moorhouse in his sublime book of Bury's suffering*.

"The rarest keepsakes of all** were locked in the memories of ageing people who had known the time of Gallipoli. They were a declining number who sometimes did not live in the town any more. Fifty miles away on the coast, where many rivers flow out of the hills into the moody shoal waters of Morecambe Bay, a white haired old lady could picture as clearly as if it had just happened, the terrifying moment when her mother collapsed at the news that her father would not be coming home from the Dardanelles. Alice Scowcroft then, she was Alice Mitchell now, with grown-up children of her own, contented secure, but marked for life by the tragedy that had overtaken her family when she was only six. The thrift that her mother Sarah had needed to practice on a widow's pension and what little else she could earn, had stood Alice in good stead when she herself was married and running a boarding house for holidaymakers from the inland towns of Lancashire: she instinctively knew about the value for money, and how not to let anything go to waste, and how to plan a domestic economy that never broke down. But there was pain, still, when she recalled her mother's suffering and devotion to the memory of James Scowcroft. The little family never could face the idea of watching the soldiers march at Gallipoli Sunday***. Instead, when Alice got married, Sarah took her bouquet after the couple had left on their honeymoon, and laid it on the War Memorial outside the Parish Church. Alice's own grief had been increasingly focused on her mother's because that did not end until the day Sarah died; and because Alice's memories of James had been so relatively short.

Her last image of him was when she came home from school and saw him walking towards her with his uniform over his arm. He was on his way back from the Drill Hall,

---

*   *Hells Foundations*, p 220-1
**   A reference to the prices fetched by VC's at auction
***This is how my grandmother must have felt.

where he'd just reported for duty with the 1st/5th, and he picked her up and gave her a big hug. After that, everything was blank. In her later years, retired and able to savour the tranquil loveliness of the estuary beside her home, Alice would occasionally remember that parting wistfully - it was now no worse than that - and wonder where her mother had got the strength to carry on. Sometimes she would go to the drawer where small things had been kept carefully, so that they could always be found: some Cairo tram tickets, a Christmas menu from the Grand Continental Hotel, and a birthday card for February 1915, with "6 hugs" beneath a big kiss in her father's hand. She would run her fingers over these fragile slips of paper and feel comforted by their touch before putting them away again. Then she would clear her throat and go to the front window, and look out to see whether the tide was running yet, and if anyone was up to his bare knees in the water, treading for flukes."

Alice's dad, James Scowcroft died on 6 June: I find the above passage heart-rending: Alice's memories survived for the future telling - my family's memories went to the grave: this illustrates better than my words the anger at the family cover-up. All the summer and for the rest of the war the *Bury Times* ran their '*Local Heroes*' picture gallery. The Ash family had to live with their grief. Other families had worse to bear. I can be certain that my grandmother had no time for the triumphalism of the 31 July item in the *Bury Times*:

"BURY OUGHT TO BE PROUD OF <u>HER SOLDIERS."</u>

Mrs. Taylor of 36 Union-Square, Bury, has received a letter from her son, Private John James Taylor of Greenhaigh Row, Freetown, a member of the 1st/5th Lancashire Fusiliers. Private Taylor, who has been wounded in the muscle, writes: "I am in the convalescent hospital at Alexandria, and have been three weeks; but I am going to the firing line tomorrow ...

I suppose you will have got word about our George and Jim (his cousin, Private J. H. Crossley, of Deal Street) by now dying out here. It is hard for me to think about them both. I saw George get hit but I had not time to think; I had to do my duty ...

I think Bury should be proud of her soldiers, for what they have done. They used to call us 'Saturday night soldiers,' but they have no need now. We have done as much as anybody in the army, perhaps more than a lot. I believe there are fellows at street corners yet. They ought to be ashamed of themselves, when lads only 15 or 16 are fighting for their country. I don't think the war will last long."

Equally, another item would give no comfort or solace:

A BUGLER'S EXPERIENCE

Bugler Tom White, 1st/5th Lancashire Fusiliers, has written home to his parents who reside at 25, Peel Street, Heywood, stating that he was wounded in the back on July 12th at the Dardanelles and was removed on a hospital ship going to Alexandria. The bullet, he says, has not come out yet. "I think," he adds, "that it will be a few weeks of a job, but you must not get alarmed. There are not many left in our battalion now. Hubert Scott and Harry Cummers are all right. There are, however, only four drummers left. We had two drummers killed on the 4 June. We have had a terrible time of it, and I can tell you I have seen some terrible sights. Don't be alarmed, I will write soon." Bugler White is 24 years of age. He has been connected with the Territorials for years. He worked as a spinner at the Plum Mill before the war. He had been connected with St. James's Church Lad's Brigade, acting as bugler. At the time of the King's visit to Lancashire, two years ago, Bugler White was chosen the King's Bugler at Bury.

On the very day, 3 July 1915, that the death on 4 June 1915 of Private George Vivian Ash was given public notice, the *Bury Guardian* published a letter from a survivor of the 4th June fighting in the Third Battle of Krithia in which he had died. Private John Riley writing on 19 June said:-

---

"I was one out of hundreds wounded during the bombardment and bayonet charge on 4th June when we took four lines of Turkish trenches, losing a lot of men **(including Private George Vivian Ash)** but the Turks must have lost six times as many as we did. Their trenches were piled with their dead; most of them were put out by shell-fire, as our artillery simply poured shells on them, and what were left had to be brought out with the bayonet."

I doubt if this is the sort of account a mother wants to read about the action in which her son died, leaving open , as it does, how he died, but the reference to 'the bayonet' brings a chill to my flesh. I hope my family never saw the War Diary of the 1st/5th Battalion as I did at the Lancashire Fusiliers Museum. The entry for 4th June gives details of several casualties and then in ten words covers with a cloak the reality of fighting on Gallipoli: *"Nos of OR* (other ranks) *casualties not obtainable for several days."* I suspect that this was a euphemism for bodies left in no-man's land.

So far, the people of Bury had only to come to terms with death on a grotesque scale. It was six months before they reconciled with defeat. Their men had been terribly let down by their leaders. The official news from Gallipoli was cloaked in an optimistic gloss, which even from the end of the first day was scarcely justified. Unofficial news accumulated slowly and lagged about a month behind the events they related. Gradually, the scale and grotesqueness of the losses became impossible to deny. Over the remaining months of 1915, the people of Bury, and East Lancashire, grew to realise that not only had their men suffered heavy losses but also had performed in the glorious style of Minden. Twelve months later, on the anniversary of the landings a memorial service was held in Bury Parish Church, as it has been every year since without exception. The ANZAC's have their ANZAC Day annual public holiday: on the nearest Sunday to 25th April Bury has its *Gallipoli Sunday*. This is what the *Bury Times* said in 1916:-

---

FUSILIER HEROES.

MEMORIAL SERVICE AT BURY PARISH CHURCH.

To commemorate the anniversary of the landing of British troops at Gallipoli, a memorial service for the officers and men of the 1st Battalion Lancashire Fusiliers who fell at Lancashire Landing, was held in the Bury Parish Church on Sunday morning. The church was crowded. The congregation included the Mayor and Mayoress ... members and officials of the Corporation, and a number of officers and soldiers from the Bury Barracks, the depot of the Lancashire Fusiliers, a contingent of the 1st/5th Battalion Lancashire Fusiliers (Territorials) who had fought on the Gallipoli peninsula ... The Mayor and members and officials of the Corporation met at the Council Offices prior to the service and walked in procession to the church ...

Among those in the church was Colonel George E. Wike. He had been wounded in the retreat from Krithia and this was the man who had spoken so warmly of Sergeant-Major Ash when he retired.

Something terribly sad happened just before the Rev. Charles Hill was due to make his address at the memorial service: he had had the dreaded telegram telling his only son had been killed on the Western Front: his wife was in despair: undaunted, but with great bravery, he delivered his address:-

---

THE RECTOR'S ADDRESS.

A few days ago, on the 25 April, a vast congregation assembled in Westminster Abbey, the most historic church in our land and indeed in the wide world. The King was there and many of his foremost subjects. The Mayor and members and officials of the

---

Corporation met at the Council Offices prior to the service and walked in procession to the church ... and more interesting even than these men of place and power, there were some 3,000 soldiers who were received with enthusiastic cheers as they passed along the streets of London. They were men who had come from the outskirts of the Empire, from Australia and New Zealand, on the call of the old motherland. They had left their homes and their occupations and they had travelled 12,000 miles to fight for freedom and honour, to offer themselves, their very souls and bodies, in the service of the land which, though few of them had ever seen it, all of them loved to call home. We know how, when they were put to the test they quitted themselves like men, how these citizen soldiers, merchants and farmers, clerks and labourers, poor students, the men of wealth, leapt, as their Prime Minister has said, unheralded into the arena of war and by their matchless courage and endurance proved themselves worthy of kinship with the most highly trained soldiers of Britain's proudest regiments of the line. They came to the famous Abbey on the anniversary of the day when they landed on the shores of Gallipoli, where in the early dawn of that fateful 25th of April they scaled heights in the face of a murderous fire, and by grit and pluck and their dash and endurance crowned themselves with glory and achieved what was impossible, but at how great a cost ? As they fought their way on and up those grim heights they had to pay full toll for every inch of ground they won, and hundreds of their bravest and best fell never to rise again in this life, but leaving an example to be imitated by generations yet unborn. And it was to commemorate those fallen warriors that their comrades made their way to the Abbey, themselves, many of them, maimed and lame, and blind and broken, and the heart of London and all Britain, aye, and of the whole Empire, went out to them in fullest sympathy as they made mention in the house of God and their fallen dead, whose glory will encircle Australia and New Zealand until time be done, and whose example will never cease to inspire all who dwell beneath the Southern Cross.

Rev Hill was speaking of the Anzacs, who in modern times, by their continuing national celebration of the glory they won at Gallipoli, have tended to monopolise the remembrance: Rev Hill knew to speak of Lancashire.

THE 1ST BATTALION LANCASHIRE FUSILIERS

But men of Lancashire, while we pay the honour that is due to those gallant ones who came from the dominions beyond the seas to fight and fall on our behalf, we don't and dare not forget the part played on that same day and on that same shore by the sons of England, Scotland, and Ireland, and, as in duty bound, we specially commemorate the immortal heroism shown by the officers and men of the 1st Battalion Lancashire Fusiliers, our own regiment, whose home is here in Bury, whose colours hang proudly in this fair church, whose memorials speak to us from our walls.

(Having said what he said of the ANZACS, Rev Hill took a breath and said what needed to be said to his congregation)

If they did not find mention in the Abbey, at least they shall find it here, for they are ours, our brothers, and our flesh, and the record of their deathless deeds is the heritage of our country and of our town for all time. Let me recall to you what Admiral De Roebeck said to them: "It is impossible to exalt too highly the services rendered by the 1st Battalion Lancashire Fusiliers in the storming of the beach. The dash and gallantry displayed were superb." A right noble tribute to our soldiers from an illustrious officer of the sister service, and a tribute right well deserved, for they achieved on that 25th April a feat of arms to which military history can scarcely afford a parallel. Under a hail of fire from hidden guns they landed from their open boats and by their dauntless courage fought their way on, though all the while losing very heavily, until the beach and the approaches to it were in their possession, to be named after them, 'Lancashire Landing' so long as Britain's Empire shall endure. We recall with pride how a signal distinction was bestowed on this battalion, unique, I believe, in the history of the British Army. For its valour three Victoria Crosses* were awarded to it, and as all had behaved themselves so gallantly, the officers and men of the Battalion were themselves entrusted with the choice of those from among themselves to whom this, the highest honour that a soldier can win, should be given. Do not our hearts thrill with pride and gratitude when we recall their splendid prowess, and are not impelled to lift up our thanks and praises to Almighty God for those brave men, alike the survivors and fallen, who

ADDED FRESH LUSTRE TO THEIR REGIMENT

and the whole British Army, and have left to all men, and most of all to us in Bury, an example of courage, tenacity, patriotism and sacrifice which ought to inspire everyone of us to live more worthily of those who have given everything, even life itself, for our sakes. "Let us then" - and here I speak words used in the Abbey on Anzac Day - "unite in praise and thanksgiving for our brothers who died at Gallipoli for their King and Country and the high cause of freedom and honour" and especially let us commemorate the officers and men of the 1st Battalion Lancashire Fusiliers, for they fought most valiantly. Their deeds will be remembered evermore, their memorial is inscribed on our hearts. in future ages sons of our country will seek to follow their example of daring and of courage. We are resolved that by God's gracious favour these our brothers shall not have laid down this, that a man lay down his life for his friends" - "leaving us an example." O God, to us may grace be given to follow in their train.

Even from the beginning the Anzacs hijacked the 25th April anniversary as their day. This was given the political nod in the highest circles in order to placate the Empire governments. But the Rev Hill was not to be denied fixing the date into the legend of the Lancashire Fusiliers. However, as I have already remarked, this did not cut any ice with my grandmother for, in the twenty two years of my life before she died, I never once heard her mention the name - Gallipoli Sunday!

---

* **Later, this was increased to six.**

In September 1919 the *Bury Times* published a commentary on the report of the Dardanelles Commission which had been appointed to investigate the causes of the disaster. With the war finished ten months earlier one can almost sense a fatigued resignation. Tucked away at the lower end of a column, there is no hint of outrage on the cost to Bury of the blunders. Reproduced below is the entire *Bury Times* report of just over 250 words. In today's world, the media would have fed on the report for a week!

WHY WE FAILED AT GALLIPOLI

COMMISSION'S FINAL REPORT

The final report of the Dardanelles Commission, issued on Monday night, is a terrible indictment of the majority of those concerned in the Gallipoli expedition. It severely criticises every aspect of the expedition-conception, maintenance, and operations. As regards the origin, the report states that between February and April no plan of operations was made, although it was known that landing was to be made, and emphasises how the naval bombardment in November gave the Turks a hint of what was coming. A supplementary report states that this bombardment was made by the Admiralty without consulting the War Council. After the first failure, General Hamilton's request for reinforcements went unheeded for several weeks, the delay being due to the political crisis caused by the formation of the Coalition Cabinet. The operations themselves and the commanders are severely criticised. General Hamilton being censured for intervening during General Stopford's attack at Suvla.

The War Office and the commanders on the spot are condemned for not having given sufficient thought to the difficulties of the task and for not having provided the expedition with the necessary men and munitions.

Even more serious are the findings contained in the Hon. Sir Thomas Mackenzie's supplementary report, which describes the "breakdown of the War Office system on the testing ground of battle" as being largely responsible for the "Gallipoli disaster". It reveals the scandal of the lack of water supplies, and quotes an officer's admission that lives had to be thrown away to "avoid the necessity of artillery preparation".

The Dardanelles Commission report is worth reading from only one point of view - it is a study in whitewash.

In 1925, on the 10th anniversary of the Lancashire Landing, the Rev Hill returned to the theme of the rightful place of the Lancashire Fusiliers. The *Bury Times* reported:-

LANCASHIRE LANDING IN GALLIPOLI

COMMEMORATION IN BURY

Saturday was the anniversary of the Lancashire Landing in Gallipoli, and on Sunday morning a commemoration service was held at the Bury Parish Church, which was attended by the Mayor (Councillor J. Hill), and members of the Town Council as well as members of the Regular and Territorial Forces. The church was crowded ...

THE SERMON

The Rev J. C. Hill ... said that the men whom they commemorated that day were the men who ten years ago carved their names by their gallantry on the cliffs of Gallipoli; the men who wrote their names with their blood on the pages of the history of our Empire. Ten years ago there came to be people of this country through the means of those pitiful, pitiless telegrams which the people ... dreaded* ... a story which thrilled them and which, as it was more and more unfolded before the eyes of their minds and imaginations, filled them increasingly with pride. There was a wonderful thing - men from the Southern lands ... who had known nothing of military history but ... showed themselves worthy of the proudest traditions of the British Army. Australia, New Zealand - we honoured them, and when a year had passed it was right and fitting that their gallant deeds should be celebrated by a service of memorial at Westminster Abbey, and we grudged nothing of that; no, nor did we grudge the fact that the 25th of April was called after them Anzac Day ... But there was something else in their hearts.

Rev Hill succeeded in concealing his own anger at the political expediency of allowing the Anzacs to hijack 25 April, but he was never going to deny Lancashire's place in the Gallipoli story. The Rev Hill asserted the rightful claim, without diminishing the Anzac right to nobility, by saying:

"Anzac Day for the Empire was
LANCASHIRE FUSILIERS DAY
for them; their men no less than those from the southern lands achieved the impossible, and Lancashire Landing stood as their memorial to all time. So while the Empire had its commemoration at Westminster Abbey, they, nine years ago, began their commemoration service there, and through the weary years of war they continued it, embracing in their hearts not only those who fought and died at Gallipoli, but those who (died) in every theatre of war ... It was fitting surely that in that church they should forge constantly, stronger links, binding them to that Regiment which gained for itself a lustre and glory surpassed - they did not hesitate to say it, nor did they fear contradiction - surpassed by no Regiment in the British Army. There, where their colours hung from the walls, they were to have - he regretted that it was not possible to say they had to-day a book of record, wherein the names of all those of the Lancashire Fusiliers who fell

---

* He had had his own telegram: he would know how pitiless were the telegrams.

in the Great War were inscribed*. Where better could such a book be placed than in the Mother Church of Bury ..."

I am left wondering if it was not only my grandmother who closed her mind to the horror of, as she called it *"The Dardanelles"*. Certainly, the tradition of *"Gallipoli Sunday"* lives on, started by the church and still actively supported by it, but something was never quite the same in Bury. The recruits flocked to volunteer, as we have seen, when war broke out in 1914. This was not to be repeated when the second war loomed. The Territorials were constantly under strength: the pain was enduring. The men of Bury did their duty when the time came but there had been too much to bear to be first in line again. I am reminded of my 1950's raconteur who told me of a scene in a pub when a group of Lancashire Fusiliers squaddies was gathered. An old woman reached out and touched the yellow hackle on the beret of one of the soldiers. *"Why did you do that ?* she was asked, to which came the unanswerable reply: *"We lost five to the Lancashire Fusiliers ! Why shouldn't I touch the hackle?"*

A German post card from a 1915 painting in celebration of the strategical victory over the Royal Navy at The Dardanelles.

* This roll of honour was produced and is in the Parish Church, and the Lancashire Fusiliers museum.

Chapter 8

"Damn the Dardanelles"

This is not a book about the fighting in Gallipoli - as the reader will be aware, it is more about the suffering of the bereaved. So far as my own bereavement is concerned - sustained in my middle age - it left me with an unrestrainable need to understand and explain to my present readers how the disaster came about. That I needed to discover how the campaign ripened into its almost mythical state can be reasoned very simply - now, it was personal. As has been related already I did not know that my grandmother's brother died at Gallipoli. Just a few months before I penned these words, all I knew was the inscription on the clock. Now that I knew that I had a relation (*"Remembered at Helles"* to quote from his Commonwealth War Graves Commission memorial) I had a cathartic need and impulse to know how it came about. But I have deliberately not attempted to write about the land campaign: there is nothing I can usefully add to what is in the literature already and the reader cannot be expected to have my special interest in the third battle of Krithia where Private Ash died. My account starts in this chapter at the beginning of the Gallipoli campaign, and in the next it ends on the morning of 25 April 1915; a day of great bravery, of VC's and, it has to be said, some dubious wisdom on the part of high ranking generals; it draws heavily on published material with some enlightenment from a previously unpublished diary.*

The curious reader, many of whom may be unaware of why and how Gallipoli came to sear its name into history, is given here a brief account of the strategic and tactical issues that create the monument of Gallipoli. In drawing together the threads of how the campaign came to be fought and how Private Ash was involved in it I have been helped by three highly rated books, all called *"Gallipoli"*. One is by Robert Rhodes James, first published in 1965, with a new edition in 1999; the second and newest by Colonel Michael Hickey (an authority on the peninsular and a member of the Gallipoli Association) whose book was published in 1995, and the third, first published in 1956, by Alan Moorehead. I have drawn material from all those works and I commend each to any reader whose quest for more understanding is unsatisfied.

Writing in 1965, some 50 years after the campaign, Moorehead makes a general observation: he recalls that the expectation of the many authors of books written in the immediate aftermath of the campaign, was that the memory of various glorious feats of arms, would last indelibly. But, he ventures, how many

---

* The unpublished diaries of Brigadier-General (later Sir) Steuart Hare. I am grateful to his grandson, David Hare, for permission to publish extracts.

remembered in 1965, the *"immortal"* names of the *Lancashire Landing, Gully Ravine* or the *Third Battle of Krithia* ? Not many then, he suggests; none now I suggest save for specialists and those growing few who want to find out more through family connections and because the Great War is more fully studied in schools. The typical stereotype is of a disaster for which Churchill was to blame. Not much more knowledge than that is typical. Even I, with my twenty-five-year-long direct exposure to Bury culture in the 1940's, 50's and 60's, had not heard of *Lancashire Landing*! I have already argued that this was probably due to the coping strategy adopted intuitively by my grandmother to contain her grief; she didn't want the memory to be immortal: I have absolutely no doubt that she wanted to extirpate the rancorous memory. Moorehead was not wrong when he said in 1965: *"Even as* (the) *names ... have almost vanished from the memory, and whether this hill was taken or that trench was lost* (it) *seems hardly to matter any more. All becomes lost in a confused impression of waste and fruitless heroism, of out of date-ness and littleness in another age"*. If that were true in 1965 how much more true is it now ? There is an irrefutable *out of dateness* about massed armies, of battle casualties in their thousands, let alone the hundreds of thousands of Gallipoli and of a volunteer army. But beware, Gallipoli is not at all out of date for military thinkers. In an age when the army is, in scale a mere scout troop compared with the massed khaki hoards of the first or even second world wars, to have an amphibious capability is axiomatic for any force to be relevant. Gallipoli was the first amphibious operation in modern times against beaches defended with modern weaponry. Surprising though it may be, the Falkland Islands were not retaken in 1982 without there being a run on remaining stocks of Rhodes James book on Gallipoli so that the lessons could be rehearsed.

In the new preface to the 1999 edition of this book, Rhodes James explains that military planners used his book to help with understanding what they were taking on in sending a naval task force, at short notice, in order to launch an invasion many thousands of miles away against defended shores in an inhospitable climate. In spite of this *"... we faithfully repeated many of the mistakes"* confessed Sir John Fieldhouse, the Commander-in-Chief, specially the reluctance of the soldiers to advance inland after the initial landings.

According to Major-General Julian Thompson, the Royal Marines commander in the Falklands War: *"Gallipoli was the first modern amphibious operation; it should be required study by Ministers, the MOD, and all staff colleges, as a warning of the perils of letting our amphibious skills wither and perish. No criticism of the way the operation was conducted by the higher command, and especially the politicians, should be allowed to tarnish the memory of the men who took part"*.*

---

* Speech to the Autumn Lunch of the Gallipoli Association 2000.

"There was considerable ignorance of the imperatives of the amphibious art in high places in particular, but also throughout the armed forces, as a result of the low priority placed on such operations by the MOD in general and the Royal Navy in particular."

So says Thompson again, but he was not speaking of Gallipoli but of the Falklands ! So perhaps we have moved on, or back perhaps, from Moorehead's observation, in 1965, of Gallipoli having or sort of *"out of dateness"*. In the conduct of military affairs it seems to have a vital relevance still, and knowledge of it reposes well with those entrusted with our political affairs as we move on into the post Cold War era of terrorism and guerrilla warfare.

There is no other battlefield quite like Gallipoli that I know. Not even Kohima,* sublime, distant, unknown even: it didn't have the extended duration (eight months) of Gallipoli. The climate at Kohima was as bad but at Gallipoli there were extremes of summer heat and winter cold and rain. There was a fanatical enemy opposing trench lines sometimes no more than a tennis court distance apart: both battles had that in common. Kohima was a turning point in the Far East War. Gallipoli proved itself neither to be critical in defeat nor, according to some, notably the historian A. J. P. Taylor, would not have been in victory. In North Africa huge distances measurable in hundreds of miles of front at a time could be abandoned without any great tactical loss before a new stand was made. At Stalingrad**, if a street was lost, there was the next building to be fought for, and the next, and so on before the next street could be fought for and lost until, if necessary, the whole city, and army, had been consumed. At Gallipoli the beachheads were so narrow that there was no ground to be given up - they were so tenuously held that if they were not held, the sea beckoned: this should not be doubted, for both sides were fighting for their lives. If the Turks had lost their hills they would have faced annihilation by shelling. In the end neither army was able to force the issue. The end came in a brilliantly organised withdrawal in which not a man gave up his life. This was no Dunkirk: it was no hastily organised improvised affair. This was sheer cunning, a meticulously crafted evacuation which was held in awe by the enemy when they realised the deception which had been perpetrated on them. Gallipoli is different. How else could an organisation like Gallipoli Association grow its membership, where no veterans survive. Many of the regiments no longer exist either, in a modern army more noted for its high level of competence than for its numbers. The second generation bred by the veterans is largely in its 70's: it is third generation interest, which is now attracted to knowledge of the campaign.

---

* The battle of Kohima was a particularly bestial affair fought to the death by the Japanese at the limit of their advance in Burmah in early 1944. It was to the Burmah campaign what Alamein was to the North African. It is largely forgotten, if ever known other than for its famous memorial.
"When you go home tell them of us and say: for your tomorrow we gave our today"
** The catastrophe for the German army which marked the turning point in the war in Russia in 1942-43.

Moorehead described the scene that newly arriving soldiers would have absorbed as they approached Cape Helles. By day in summer it was a pleasant trip across a blue sea until about five miles out they would have seen that the land was overhung by a yellowish cloud of dust and soon "*... a sickly carrion smell came out across the sea ...*" and a fringe of decaying rottenness lay along the shore. Dust covered everything, shells came crashing through it and the soldiers endured it as a natural part of life. As summer arrived, then came the flies and they stayed, bloated and gorging until winter. Everyone who was at Gallipoli mentions the flies. There was no respite even when night fell. "It was a plague of such pestilence and foulness it was a wonder men didn't go mad in their helplessness. *"The flies fed on the unburied corpses in no man's land, and on the latrines, the refuse and the food of both armies."* A. P. Herbert, the playwright, author and MP, who served in Gallipoli, wrote these lines:-

> *"The flies! Oh, God, the flies*
> *That soiled the sacred dead.*
> *To see them swarm from dead men's eyes*
> *And share the soldiers' bread.*
> *Nor think I now forget*
> *The filth and stench of war,*
> *The corpses on the parapet*
> *The maggots on the floor"*

Need I write more ? Disease followed and was soon to cause heavy attrition in the line. As autumn came there was the coldness and the rain to endure, and for the wounded if respite came it was only after an age of suffering, not for want of compassion, save for those trapped in no-man's land, but for medical resources. But we are getting ahead of ourselves.

Why were the soldiers going to Gallipoli? At this distance it seems remarkable that Britain should be at war with Turkey at all. Not since the crusades had Britons fought Turks. More recently, in the mid nineteenth century, Britain allied itself with Turkey against Tsarist Russian expansion intrigues over the declining Ottoman Empire. This led to the Anglo-French-Turkish war against Russia in the Crimea of 1853 to 1856. This war was a culmination of a long series of wars between Russia and Turkey at whose core lay the control over the Dardanelles; a 38 mile strait separating Europe from Asia and connecting the Mediterranean and Black Seas. It has been strategically significant throughout history, the strait being crucial to the wealth of ancient Troy, the security of Constantinople (the former name of Istanbul) and Russian access to the warm water seas. As Napoleon said in 1808:-

"Who is to have Constantinople ? That is always the crux of the problem".

It is interesting to note that the Crimean War arose because of a British rejection of Russian proposals for a more or less Anglo-Russian dismemberment of the Ottoman Empire (Turkey being dubbed 'the Sick Man of Europe'). In fact, the Russian proposals had considerable attractions:-

"The Turks with their record of massacre and outrage, deserved no consideration ... By the Tsar's plan the Christian races of south-east Europe would be freed from the intolerable menace under which they were living. The plan (for dismemberment) *could have been carried out without a great deal of fighting. Some other European powers would have objected, but they would have hesitated to attack a combination of the Russian Army and the British Navy, both reputed to be the strongest in Europe. Turkish resistance was to be expected, but it could hardly have been successful."* *

In a speech delivered by Lloyd George, he expressed the opinion that had Britain come to terms with the Tsar at this time, five wars would have been averted. There would have been no Crimean War, no Russo-Turkish War in 1877-8; it is possible that the Balkan Wars of 1912-13 would not have taken place and that even the Great War of 1914-18 might have been averted. Russia and Great Britain would have become firm allies, and British interests need not have been endangered by Russian access to the Mediteranean.

That Russia needed supplies through the straits, when war broke out in 1914 gave vivid colour to the Dardanelles status as a fulcrum for war-making minds. On this occasion it was German intriguing which got the better of British attempts to keep Turkey out of the war she did not join until three months after the outbreak.

During the summer of 1914, two German cruisers, *Goeben* and *Breslau* had been showing the flag ostentatiously in the eastern Mediterranean and at Constantinople as part of the Kaiser's policy of wooing the 'young Turks' who had gained control of Turkey the previous year. At this time, Turkey had two Super-Dreadnoughts building in Britain. On 2 August 1914 these ships, nearing completion, were impressed into the Royal Navy. Whatever the strategic naval imperatives for this action were (and they were self evident for a nation which survived on naval supremacy or at the worst, equality with its enemies) its arbitrary handling played into the hands of the German intriguer. Their public relations coup was sealed when the announcement of the taking of the warships, without compensation, was made. At this distance, it seems to have been particularly stupid to have made no attempt to sugar the pill**. It takes a particular arrogance to behave in such a unilateral, unthinking way and a complete ignorance of the fact that actions create reactions! A big price was to be paid for this clumsiness.

---

* England 1783-1914 by G. W. Southgate: 1951, p.139.
** At the eleventh hour Churchill made attempts to trade compensation for the quitting of the German crews from the *Goeben* and *Breslau*, but it was too late. A state of war had been set on an irreversible course.

Meanwhile the *Goeben* and the *Breslau* slipped out of Constantinople on a raiding party in the Mediterranean. After evading the Royal Navy they sailed back through the Dardanelles in defiance of treaties in force at the time (Germany being a belligerent at war, Turkey being neutral) and back to Constantinople. Shortly after this, the vessels were given by Germany to Turkey to compensate for the confiscation of the two warships by Britain. Cheap at the price!

In January 1915, after Turkey had entered the war, Imperial Russia appealed to Britain and France for help against Germany. Churchill, as First Lord of the Admiralty, over-rode the advice of his First Sea Lord, Fisher, and persuaded the Cabinet to sanction a naval expedition to force its way to Constantinople and to eliminate Turkey from the war. Initially, the talk was about an expedition; the idea was pushed first this way, then that, without consistent central control, and it ended up as a campaign. This is a key point: Churchill got the blame for it. Certainly it was his idea. But he was not in control. Right from the start no one person or representative group was in control. At times the venture was on the brink of victory but it ended in unalloyed defeat; the naval losses were affordable but the huge loss of British, Australasian, Indian and French life was not. Much *matériel* was lost as well as life for no gain other than the slaughter of huge swathes of the Turkish army and considerable loss to her shipping. It saw the end of volunteer armies, the emergence into full statehood of Australia and New Zealand* and the creation of the foundations of modern Turkey. The luckless fighting men did their best but were *'beaten in the end by our own leaders'*. There was to be heroism on an epic scale but with huge suffering, on all sides. The suffering in the Crimean War (which became well reported) came with victory; the suffering at Gallipoli came with defeat: the seeds of the disaster were to be sown early.

In early 1915 military resources were scarce. Powerful lobbies existed for avoiding removing troops from the Western Front in France. This contributed materially to the push me/pull you gestation of the offensive stroke against the Dardenelles; moreover, it lead to the compromise notion of a unilateral naval answer to questions of how to force the straits. This was to appease the lobby that did not wish to spare troops for a non-critical front. No matter that the compromise flew in the face of high-level military analysis, which before the war, had delivered a highly articulate report which highlighted the impossibility of success by naval action alone. Thus was the compromise flawed! The 1906 report by the director of naval intelligence and the general staff concluded that:-

---

* As the ANZAC forces they made, in their exploits on the ANZAC beach and later in holding the beach head, the first indelible statement that either of the two young countries had made to the world. Unlike Lancashire (or any where else in the home country) the statement became indelible. Even in 2001 the Australian cricket team went out of its way to visit Gallipoli on its way to England for its cricket tour in order to establish a bonding experience.

"Success must be certain. A mere naval raid (through the Dardanelles) *... being a dangerous and ineffective operation the work will have to be undertaken by a joint naval and military expedition having for its objective the capture of the Gallipoli peninsula and destruction of the forts which at present deny entrance to ... these waters."*

The report continued with great insight:-

"The successful conclusion of a military operation against the Gallipoli peninsula must hinge on the ability of the fleet ... to dominate the Turkish defences with gunfire and to crush their field troops during that period of helplessness which exists while an army is in the actual process of disembarkation, but also to cover the advance of the troops once ashore, until they could gain a firm foothold and establish themselves upon the high ground in rear of coast defences of the Dardanelles."

Precisely, this is what didn't happen. You couldn't write the warning better if you had seen it all going wrong nine years later.

There seemed to be an explicit agreement among the top military strategists that *"unaided fleet action was to be deprecated"*. According to Hickey* *"this crucial report was duly passed from department to department, initialled and filed away. Nobody gave any thought to any possible requirement for a joint service command structure as a result of it"*. This is dynamite ! What it means is that some sharp military brains had sat down, thought about the problem calmly, and concluded that the Dardanelles could not be taken except by a task-force of naval and military resources acting in concert. As we will see, it was not to be. Churchill knew but according to Lloyd George: *"The Dardanelles failure was due not so much to Mr. Churchill's precipitancy as to Lord Kitchener's and Mr. Asquith's procrastination."* Respectively, these were the senior soldiers, now in the Government as Secretary of State and the Prime Minister.

Hickey's account continues by discussing a highly accurate intelligence report and assessment of the Turkish defences, which the British Military Attaché, Lieutenant-Colonel F. Cuncliffe-Owen, at Constantinople had sent to the War Office in September 1914. Its timing was fortuitous but its contents were ignored. He pointed out that Turkish defences were growing appreciatively stronger as the result of energetic German effort including the supply of artillery (from Krupps). He pointed out that there were more profitable areas where Turkey could be attacked (Persian Gulf, along the Red Sea or Syria) and where it would be impossible to reinforce her garrisons in the face of overwhelming Royal Navy superiority.   These 'cheap' prizes were nothing of course to those, led by Churchill, who wanted the knock-out blow to take Turkey out of the war by opening up the Dardanelles. In the end we did not get the knock-out; huge human and *matériel* losses were suffered and the Gallipoli legend and myths were

---

* *Gallipoli*, Michael Hickey: p. 28.

born.

If the Dardanelles were to be opened permanently, concluded Cunliffe-Owen, military force would have to be applied on the Gallipoli peninsula before the navy could proceed with confidence through the straits. This authoritative analysis, it may amaze the reader, did not prevent a unilateral attempt by the Royal Navy to blast its way through; an attempt which was to fail!

More surprisingly, according to Hickey, and here is the smoking gun:-

"Although Cuncliffe-Owen's report was circulating in Whitehall in October 1914, neither it nor the joint services report of 1906 was produced in 1915 when the Mediterranean Expeditionary Force was launched, and its commander Sir Ian Hamilton was not even aware of their existence when he left London in March 1915 to assume command of the force."

This can scarcely be credited! Well might Lord Fisher, the First Sea Lord offer his curse: *"Damn the Dardanelles - they will be our grave !"* My grandmother and Lord Fisher would have got on very well! The situation now was that the campaign would gestate without a single leader or group in control and the project has embraced the very unilateral naval approach that the leaders should have been told, or were already aware, was considered, after unhurried analysis, to be unsound.

The fleet which the Royal Navy, with its French allies, had assembled in the Mediterranean was the greatest concentration of naval strength which that sea had ever seen. No matter that some of the heavy ships were obsolete and due to be scrapped; some fourteen battleships and dozens of lesser warships and attendant vessels were under the command of Admiral Carden who flew his flag in HMS *Queen Elizabeth*, a brand new 15 inch gun battleship fresh from the builders. The fleet had total control of the Mediterranean; no force dare assail it*. Admiral Carden was induced by Churchill to develop a plan to take the Dardanelles by unilateral naval action (in spite of the refined wisdom in top military minds that it couldn't be done without troops)! Carden's brute force plan was developed in response to a request by Churchill, and was not as a self-justifying enterprise by the Royal Navy to take the Dardanelles on its own. It had as its first part, a deliberate bombardment at stand-off range followed by medium and very close range naval gunfire. Under cover of bombardment, minesweepers were to clear the channel at its entrance. The attack commenced on 19 February and after a break for bad weather, was re-commenced on 25 February.

---

* A German U-Boat left Wilhelmshaven on the North Sea on 25 April, by coincidence the day of the invasion. When it arrived off Helles four weeks later it caused panic among the fleet.

Raiding parties of Royal Marines and from the Royal Naval Division were put ashore to blow up abandoned guns which naval fire had knocked out. They were no more able, however, than was the Royal Navy to knock-out the mobile guns which continued to harass the minesweeping activity and, indeed, to completely derange the resolution of their civilian crews. (In large part they were requisitioned fishing vessels from British waters now trawling for mines, not fish !)*   The essential conundrum was this: the minesweepers could not go for-ward until the guns were silenced and the battleships could not get near enough to silence the remaining guns until the mines were cleared: nerves were fraying; Admiral Carden was ill; the Turks had not been blasted away; the shooting wasn't always very accurate. Everyone had forgotten the wisdom of a few years earlier, which persisted in the view that the job couldn't be done by sea power alone. All that had been achieved so far of lasting effect was to alert the Turks (and their German commanders) that the Allies had the Dardanelles on their list of strategic goals. Their loss would mean the fall of Constantinople and Turkey with it; there was no argument about that. The Turks had no need to work out the consequences of their failure. It was their homeland that was at stake and they would have to fight for it or lose it. They were on notice it was to be attacked. From such a cause would come a fanatical defence.

For the Turks to be ruined was one thing; whether the fall of Turkey would have materially damaged Germany (which was received wisdom at the time) is questioned by eminent historians:-

A.J.P. Taylor wrote:**

"It is a mystery why most people, then and since, assumed that the fall of Constantinople would lead to the defeat of Germany. The only immediate gain would be to open a line of supply to Russia, and this gain was entirely theoretical since neither Great Britain nor France had, at this time, supplies to send. Turkey might have been knocked out of the war, but this would have lessened the burden on Germany. An Army would have had no light task to march from Constantinople to Central Europe and, in any case there was no army to spare."

This searing analysis shows that the strategic loss of resources, human and *matériel*, suffered by Great Britain and her allies in the Gallipoli campaign was a poor trade. It is starkly supportive of those contemporary minds that abhorred the diminution of resources for France where the war they claimed - and they were right in the end - would be won or lost. It is sometimes argued that the February attack was flawed because it revealed the strategic objective in the

---

* I am reminded of a Second World War veteran of my acquaintance who could never resist, when asked;"*What was it like in the war*" the dead pan answer: "*Bloody dangerous !*"
* *English History 1914 - 1945* by A.J.P. Taylor. 1965.

Allies' prosecution of the war against Turkey. I don't think there is much in this point because an earlier, somewhat petulant, bombardment had taken place the previous November; this surely was the calling card.* I am more attracted to the Cuncliffe-Owen line: a strategic deception that reinforced what Turkey expected i.e. an attack on the Dardanelles, would have facilitated cheap victories against the Turkish army elsewhere while tying up large forces of enemy troops in Gallipoli.

A further large-scale naval penetration was scheduled for 18 March. It was a fateful day in the history of the campaign. It brought an unexpected tactical victory for the Turks achieved by the laying, secretly, of a new minefield in that part of the Narrows where they had observed the big ships manoeuvring in previous attacks. It was to be a day of heavy naval losses for no perceptible gain to justify them; at least that was how it seemed to faint hearts. First, the French battleship *Bouvet* sank in minutes from a heavy explosion. The cause of this ship being sent to the bottom was unknown at the time; it was unnervingly mysterious. It had, of course fallen victim to the new minefield. Nonetheless, heavy fire was poured into the Turkish batteries and many fell silent, but the minesweepers did not press home their task. Other ships hit mines and limped away to sink later; some were crippled and fell under Turkish gunfire.

There had been a major onslaught on the Turkish batteries, but on account of the success of their mobile guns and the surprise of their new minefield, they won the day. The Royal Navy called off its attack for the day but, in fact, it was never to be resumed unilaterally. What was at the time a tactical withdrawal turned out to be a defeat. Here was the moment a supreme commander, if he had existed, would have made the difference.**

The reasons why the attempt by the Royal Navy to force the Dardanelles was abandoned after the engagement of 18 March are complicated but in large measure due to the emotional effect on the admirals of having lost great ships and the thought of hazarding yet more. Vice-Admiral de Roebeck, who had taken over from the ill Carden, lost his nerve.

In the words of Winston Churchill looking back: *"The terrible 'ifs' build up".* Of course, 'if' Russia had not put in its plea for a diversionary attack in the East there would have been no political will for the campaign in the first place, given the pressure from France for resources. Another 'if' to emerge on 18 March, but one which appears not to have galvanised any high level thought or analysis, is the profit and loss account of the exchange and consumption of resources by each side in war. A battle is won when the side who has the will to do so builds up

---

* This was the time to take the Dardanelles cheaply. The more time went by, especially after the February attacks, the greater were the defensive preparations and so, growing exponentially the heavier the hammer blow needed to be successful.
** Of course a supreme commander wouldn't have attempted what military wisdom said couldn't be done. If the objective had been set to capture the Gallipoli peninsular, then an amphibious operation would have been planned *ab initio*.

and brings to bear his offensive resources at a faster rate, or more effectively, than his enemy. The Royal Navy's losses were not in any way life threatening; even if they were regrettable in terms of ships, they were not irreplaceable and the losses of crews were not high. But losing ships is not what admirals think they are for! So far, the exchange had been of three obsolete battleships for the greater part of the whole defensive stock of artillery shells. At this rate of exchange, whole campaigns can be won!

The Turk's position as the sun went down on 18 March, as regards ammunition, was critical. The consumption of shells had been prodigious and, if continued, would have been ruinous. They had defended well; the German commanders had made an impact. But the awful reality of the worrisome arithmetic would not yield; shells were being consumed at a rate far faster than they could be re-supplied. The commanders knew that a point would come when the last shell had been fired and then! And then they could do nothing but retire. It wasn't as if it was the Turk's alone who knew of their critical position. On 15 March a signal from Berlin to Constantinople was intercepted by the British: it revealed that the Dardanelles forts were short of ammunition. The events of 18 March evidently overcame, or were allowed to overcome, the startling truth that the continuing expenditure of shells by the Turks was capable of granting an unexpected victory to the fleet. A strong commander in charge of all the resources would not have overlooked this vital intelligence. No-one in the field sat down and confronted the issue which had the vital immediacy: what tactics can we adopt which will encourage the Turks to consume their shells with least loss to ourselves ? It was only Churchill, ever quick to spot a chance, who, appraised of the intelligence report, signalled De Roebeck:-

"This (intelligence report) *agrees with our information, and importance of forcing forts to fire as often and as long as possible, in order to exhaust their ammunition, will doubtless have occurred to you. I have consulted Lord Fisher before sending this telegram, but you are free to act as you may think fit, so I mark this telegram personal, as intention of all we say is merely to be helpful and a guide, and not a hard and fast instruction."* *

According to Gilbert, and consistently with what we have seen of de Roebeck's nervousness, he had no intention of putting his ships in danger. It is not without irony, for those inclined to blame Churchill for his assertiveness, that if he had been more confident, more willing to instruct de Roebeck, the opportunity for a cheap victory might have been presented itself.

The Turks knew nothing of the alarm among the admirals caused by the losses to mines that had been caused that day. They expected the Royal Navy to return next day. But they didn't and just when victory could have been won,

---

* *Winston S. Churchill,* by Martin Gilbert, Volume 111, 1914 - 1916: 1971.

because the Turks were near to collapse through exhaustion of ammunition, the pressure on the throat was relaxed. Goering made the same mistake in 1940 when he stopped bombing RAF fighter stations! And he lost the Battle of Britain as a result. At such pivotal points, the history of the world changes.

It should be recalled that wise senior naval opinion had already opined that forcing the Dardanelles was a job that couldn't be done by the navy alone. It is perverse to realise that, on account of the Turk's ammunition position, they had almost been proved wrong. Now we had a military commander for the land forces on the spot, General Sir Ian Hamilton, who had observed the navy's difficulties in the 18 March attacks from de Roebeck's flagship, HMS *Queen Elizabeth*, and who now lent his voice to a change of tactics i.e. to resume the attack in conjunction with an invasion of the Gallipoli peninsula, not, as would have been ruinous for the Turks, to induce them to fire off all their shells.

Chapter 9

Gallipoli

In the last chapter we saw how the naval prelude had evolved. The new com-mander of the land forces had now arrived in the war zone but unlike General Wolseley, who had his plan for the invasion of Egypt in 1882 all worked out before he left England (as we saw in Chapter 6), Hamilton arrived with no plan at all! As we shall see, that had to be worked out later. This is not so much a crit-icism of him - he had only been appointed a few days before - but it illustrates colourfully, and tragically, how the whole structure of the enterprise was being built using unstable scaffolding.

To quote Rhodes James:-

"And thus, by the end of March, three months since the project had first been seriously discussed, the decision to undertake a combined operation had been taken, not by the Cabinet or the War Council, but by Hamilton and De Roebeck. The exact nature of the operations had not been defined, and never was defined. Hamilton and De Roebeck were themselves under a misapprehension. Hamilton assumed that the operations to be undertaken by his army were to be in conjunction with another naval assault on the Dardanelles, De Roebeck, however, had made up his mind that his ships would not again attack the forts until the army had occupied the Gallipoli peninsula. The fatal weakness of the divided command of the Gallipoli campaign was already becoming dimly apparent."

A serious misunderstanding was developing between Hamilton and De Roebeck about the landing. Rhodes James puts it like this:-

"Hamilton's plans were based on De Roebeck's Admiralty telegram ... that 'directly the army is landed on the Peninsula the fleet will renew its attacks on the Narrows ... No matter where the army effects its landings, the extreme objective of both Services must be the forts at the Narrows, and the intention is to attack them simultaneously with all our forces'. Hamilton interpreted this to mean that as soon as his army was ashore the Fleet would resume its aggressive assault on the Narrows, this time supported by the army on the Peninsula, providing the Turks with a double thrust at their heart. In 1924 an American historian commented that: 'Certainly General Hamilton did not suspect that naval co-operation would be so limited, and to a large extent his plans during the follow-ing month were based ... on the assumption of a combined attack with the Fleet'. In the margin Hamilton wrote:- 'Correct'."

In May, after the land battle was bogged down, the Royal Navy lost several capital ships to a German submarine, which had made the voyage from Germany. In full view of the fighting troops, the navy withdrew; they left the theatre never to return. A depression fell on the allied troops.

According to Rhodes James, Kitchener had been a too-willing recipient of Churchill's glowing enthusiasm and confidence about a naval operation. His account tells us that on 16 February Kitchener:-

"... summoned Captain Wyndham Deedes who had served with the Turkish Army and who was now working at the War Office as an intelligence officer, to seek his views on the prospects of a purely naval attack on the Dardanelles. Deedes said that the operation was fundamentally unsound, but when he began to develop his arguments Kitchener turned on him angrily, told him he did not know what he was talking about, and signified that the interview was at an end."

This was a bullying act that blinkered Kitchener as much as it must have stung Deedes. Rhodes James tells us that, nine months later when the facts spoke in Deedes' favour, Kitchener went out of his way to apologise.

Quite apart from military wisdom, which was lacking at the highest levels, there were organisational issues that were set off on the wrong foot. It is amazing, at this distance, that no one in London (Kitchener?) had thought that an amphibious operation with no overall commander is a managerial nonsense. This mistake was not made in Normandy in 1944, or the Falklands in 1982 either. That it was made in 1915 had very bad consequences and it adds to the mounting 'ifs'. When Kitchener appointed Hamilton as Commander of what was to be known as the Mediterranean Expeditionary Force, the whole Middle East theatre had three separate commands: there was a commander of the forces in Egypt (of which Private Ash was part), with responsibility for defending that country and, of course, the Suez Canal; a commander in charge of the fleet and, as we have seen, a commander for the expeditionary force. This was an organisational lapse by Kitchener of such fundamental character that one is surprised the finger has not been pointed at him as demandingly as was his at British manhood in his famous recruiting poster! Wolseley was under no such disadvantage in the Egyptian campaign of 1882; Montgomery and his 8th Army in North Africa had General Alexander in charge as Middle East theatre commander and, of course, Eisenhower was Supreme Commander of the allied naval, land and air forces invasion of Normandy, i.e. the whole show. How could it be otherwise ? Of the many people in high office at the time of Normandy, there were many who had first hand experience of the Gallipoli failure: among these Churchill, of course, but Clement Atlee, the deputy Prime Minister had served in Gallipoli himself.

So, as the preliminary phase of the Dardanelles campaign came to a close, we have this position. All hope of strategic surprise was lost, at the latest, by the February attacks by the navy. Organisational flaws were set up *ab initio*. The seeds of a logistical nightmare at the expeditionary force island base of Lemnos (with its shortage of water and woefully inadequate facilities, especially for the wounded) had been sown. All military analysis and wisdom that existed before the war had concluded that the navy, alone, could not force the Dardanelles. The First Sea Lord, Fisher, didn't want to do it and became estranged from Churchill over it. The resignation of both came when things went wrong. Churchill recovered, of course, but Fisher was too old. He had been right but not voluble enough early enough to prevent the disaster gaining its accumulating momentum. The admirals had been persuaded to try the unilateral naval penetration; they quailed over their losses and withdrew when with perseverance they might have done it - just to confound pre-war wisdom, which was ignored anyway!

Until the beginning of February all plans were made in the light of Kitchener's repeated statements, on account of pressures in France, that no troops could be made available for the Dardanelles. But pressure was being put on Kitchener and he began to waver. According to Rhodes James:-

"He had at his disposal in England a magnificent division, the 29th Division, not yet committed to any theatre."

Controversy raged over how this crack division* should be deployed. Political forces ebbed and flowed; thin ends of wedges were driven. On 16 February, Ministers agreed to send the 29th Division to the Greek island of Lemnos in the Aegean Sea; moreover the Australian and New Zealand Army Corps (ANZAC), presently in Egypt, were sent to the same place.

Although no actual decision had been made on their use in support of the fleet, these forces were to be concentrated in the Turk's back yard awaiting deployment. Rear Admiral Wemyss was instructed to proceed to Lemnos to make arrangements for the arrival and accommodation of the army. He received no inkling of the harsh fact that this island was utterly undeveloped and, apart from a very good natural harbour, had no facilities (or water) to accommodate an army. Strategy was being developed on the hoof. The pressures were forced upon the high players from all sides. The Turks could not mistake the threat. In the brutal words of Sir William Robertson (Chief of the Imperial General Staff) at the time:-

---

* It contained the 1st Battalion, Lancashire Fusiliers as part of the 86th Brigade led by Brigadier-General Hare (the grandfather of David Hare from the Foley Arms).

"The Secretary of State for War was aiming at decisive results on the Western Front; the First Lord of the Admiralty was advocating a military expedition to the Dardanelles; the Secretary of State for India was devoting his attention to a campaign in Mesopotamia; the Secretary of State for the Colonies was occupying himself with several small wars in Africa; and the Chancellor of the Exchequer was attempting to secure the removal of a large part of the British Army from France to some eastern mediterranean theatre."

On 10 March, the day of Sergeant-Major Ash's funeral, Kitchener decided to commit the 29th Division to an attack and, after a famous parade in front of King George V, it sailed for Lemnos. On 11 March he appointed General Sir Ian Hamilton as commander in chief of the Mediterranean Expeditionary Force. The resources available to him were to be the 29th Division, the Anzacs, the Royal Naval Division and a French Corps totalling over 70,000 men.

So, just before the Royal Navy's push on 18 March, we now had an army on its way; a commander for it, who had now arrived in time to watch the failed naval attack on the Dardanelles but with no plan for the use of his army; the seeds of logistical chaos and water shortage on Lemnos were already sown and the enemy had been alerted to the probability of an invasion of the Gallipoli peninsula. Brigadier-General Hare's diary is intriguing in its references to the water problem. On 24 March, having arrived in Valetta with his Brigade and after an evening ashore, Hare:-

"Did not get on board till nearly 12. Found coaling going on. It went on all night but I slept through it more or less peacefully." The next day: *"Still coaling so went to the Club for breakfast. Had a conversation with Flag Captain re getting the Mercian* (the Brigade transport) *... under way as soon as possible, as there is little ventilation between decks in harbour. He said that she would go at 5 p.m. to-day. (She did not go). He explained that the necessity for filling up with coal was not for any steaming that had to be done, but for condensing purposes."*

It was dawning on Hare that there was a problem:-

"That sounds as if what I heard yesterday is true that the island where we expect to land and get sorted out is short of water ... Came on board soon after 3 and found them still coaling on both sides. Awful mess. Don't believe we shall get off to-night. Atmosphere below awful."

The fact that Lemnos was so inadequate as an expeditionary base, except for its good natural harbour, was to be a major blemish on the campaign planning; it wasn't just the shortage of water. The gross under estimate of the casualties and the resources needed to succour them was to become a disgrace.

According to Rhodes James, in London, only Sir Maurice Hankey* seems to have had any premonition of disaster. In a memorandum discussed by the War Council on March 19th, he urged the appointment of a technical naval and military committee - the first germ of the subsequent chiefs of staff committees - *"so as to avoid repetition of the naval fiasco, which is largely due to inadequate Staff preparation"*. The paper was only perfunctorily discussed, and no action was taken. Hankey returned to the point with a memorandum to Asquith, asking that at least the objectives of the operations should be established, so that a proper appreciation of the forces needed to carry them out could be made. *"Up to the present time, so far as I am aware,"* Hankey wrote, *"no attempt has been made to estimate what Force is required to make sure of success. We have merely said that so many troops are available, and that they ought to be enough."* This is penetrating stuff. As Rhodes James observes: *"Hankey had, of course, put his finger on the fundamental defect in the whole enterprise, but his warnings went unheeded."* When he told Churchill that at least the landings would be *"of extraordinary difficulty"*, Churchill remarked: *"that we could not see that there was any difficulty at all"*. Rhodes James continues: *"In a last attempt, Hankey sent Asquith another memorandum on April 12th,"* which concluded: *"The military operation appears,therefore, to be to a certain extent a gamble upon the supposed shortage of supplies and inferior qualities of the Turkish armies."* The War Office estimated the likely casualties for landing and capturing the Peninsula at about 5,000: this was grotesquely wrong. *"At the outset,"* as the Dardanelles Commission subsequently commented, *"all decisions were taken and provisions based on the assumption that, if a landing were effected, the resistance would be slight and the advance rapid. Optimism and enthusiasm, although great military qualities, had been carried ... to an unreasoning myopia."*

So, the 29th Division was on its way and, seemingly, in very confident mood. We have to keep reminding ourselves that life in 1915 is in many ways unrecognisable today. Brigadier-General Hare's diary entries, when his transport stopped at Valletta in Malta, illuminate for us the life of an officer in those days. On 24 March his diary reads:-

"Went ashore with Farmar (Staff Captain) ... Went to Palace and wrote names in the Governor's book and Farmar who had once been an ... A.D.C. here showed us all over the Palace ... Went to the Club and had lunch. Got an invitation to dine with the Governor ... Worth being Governor to live in such a nice place. After dinner music by some of the Opera Company. Very nice and not over my head." The next day: *"went to the Club for breakfast. After breakfast wrote letters ... Lunch at the Palace. At 5 o'clock heard we*

* Sir Maurice Hankey (later Lord), Secretary to the War Council. During the 1930's he was Secretary to the Cabinet. He was one of a small number of senior civil servants and politicians who performed well in the face of the German menace in the 1930's. Later, he served in the Government during the Second World War .

are not off till 7 a.m. next morning, so went ashore again. Dined at the Club and went to the Opera ... Faust, very good.

This is a man on his way to battle, but the social round continued. When he was in Alexandria he tells us that at his dining table was Captain Roston: *"(late of the Carpatian) who rescued the Titanic survivors"* ... some three years earlier. He must have been quite a celebrity.

Even before the invasion started on 25 April 1915 decisive influences were at work. The Turkish victory of 18 March gave them a new spirit of self-belief. The respite after the naval battle gave them time to organise their defences of the Gallipoli peninsula.   A German, General Liman von Sanders, became commander of all the forces at the Dardanelles, he was to be brilliantly success-ful. Emboldened by their victory, the Turks prepared to defend their homeland, their own way of life, for without victory there was no survival. Of course, the Turks had to guess where the invasion might come and exactly when; of the certainty that it was going to come there was no doubt.

Hamilton's plan, though complicated in its details, amounted to a simple, crude even, assault upon the Gallipoli peninsula itself, with, as he put it: *"a running jump with both feet together."* According to Rhodes James, Hamilton calculated that von Sanders, the German Commander, would not dare to concentrate his forces for at least forty-eight hours after the invasion, by which time, he hoped, the decisive battle should have been fought and won. *"The whole operation was based on the reasonable assumption that the only really hazardous part of the operation was actually getting ashore, and that once this was achieved it would merely be a matter of rolling up the Turks and eliminating pockets of resistance."* I am not sure how Rhodes James rates this assumption as reasonable! What about occupying high ground quickly ? Rhodes James concedes that: *"No emphasis was ... laid in the orders to the 29th Division on the vital importance of moving inland rapidly after the disembarkation."* The orders were, he claims, excessively vague on the really important points. This was a lapse of breathtaking significance. The invasion forces were never to get more than a finger-grip on the Gallipoli peninsular.

The main landing force was to be the 29th Division, under Lieutenant-General Hunter-Weston. It was to go ashore on five small beaches at Cape Helles at the extreme tip of the peninsula, and it was hoped that by the end of the first day key high ground, six miles inland, would be taken. Meanwhile Lieutenant-General Birdwood was to land with the Anzac force about thirteen miles away on the west coast of the peninsular. Striking across the peninsula he was to cut off the Turks fighting the 29th Division at Cape Helles in their rear, and occupy the hills dominating the Narrows.

Two main diversionary attacks were to be carried out. The Royal Naval Division was to make a feint at the north end of the peninsular on its west side.

The French were to go ashore for a large armed raid on the Asiatic or east side of the Straits. Later these two forces would be brought back to Cape Helles and put into the main attack. By the second or the third day it was hoped (the whole plan was long on hope and short on estimation of the enemy) that the lower half of the peninsula would be so overrun that the Fleet with its minesweepers could safely pass through the Narrows.

This is how Brigadier-General Hare's diary describes the build up to the invasion:

April 6th. Brigade inspected by Sir Ian Hamilton, C. in C. Had not seen him for 20 years. Looks wonderfully young ... Got orders for embarkation without giving dates ... Reading between the lines the Brigade is evidently to be the covering force. (For the landings at Cape Helles)

April 8th. Division sent a motor to take ... me and our Brigade Majors to a Pow Wow at Divisional H.Q. at 10 a.m. The General could not tell us anything very definite as to operations, but anyhow the 86th Brigade is to be the Covering Force (i.e. first ashore to cover the landing of the main force) *and I hope we shall land where I always thought would be the place, namely the end of the Gallipoli Peninsula near Cape Helles.* (This is exactly where he did land) *He also removed my fears of a night landing which had been talked of and which I was convinced would be asking for trouble ...*

April 11th. ... Reached mouth of harbour at Lemnos about noon and came a short way in and anchored ... Harbour full of ships. Men of War including Queen Elizabeth (General Hamilton's headquarters), *transports, colliers, etc. Dropped anchor alongside an Australian transport. One of our men shouted, "Who are you?" The answer was "Australians. Who are you?" To which our man answered, "Soldiers". Not very tactful perhaps ...* (But very witty!) *Just before reaching the mouth of the harbour we made out what must have been the Gallipoli Peninsula. Samothrace* (an island near the Turkish Asiatic mainland) *sticks up very high to the North and has streaks of snow on it. After dinner got a message that the Queen Elizabeth was going to the Gallipoli Peninsula in the morning and would take Generals, Staff and C.O.'s.*

April 12th. Had breakfast about 7 and about 7.30 a launch came for us. First person I met on going on board was Deedes who is Intelligence Officer on G.H.Q. Staff. (This was, presumably, the Captain Deedes who had had the temerity to tell Kitchener that Carden's unilateral naval plan was fundamentally unsound. The diary entry suggests more than a passing acquaintance with Hare but there is no reference to Deedes having expressed any scepticism about the campaign.) *Sir Ian was on board and several of his Staff. All my C.O.'s and a lot of Australians. There must have been 30 or 40 of us. Q.E. well worth seeing herself. When going 23 knots one could hardly tell she was moving. Ran over to off Cape Teke in about 2 hours. Then steamed up the*

West coast of the peninsula about 2 miles out as far as Cape Suvla and turned. Had lunch about this period. We steamed back rather nearer in, about 2000 yards. After lunch one of the officers took me up to the fighting top where one sees very much better. Got a very good idea of the coast and landing places and of the country inland. It is much more open than I expected. (It is difficult to interpret this; Hare makes it sound almost straightforward) *Turned round Cape Helles till we could see as far up as the beginning of the Narrows. While we were doing this two or three shells were fired at us but did not drop within 500 yards of us. While going astern we got the benefit of the smoke on the top from the fore funnel. It was stifling. She burns oil fuel and it smelt like a thousand smoking lamps, but they say coal smoke chokes one much more. Steamed close in shore near ruins of Troy* (off the Asiatic coast) *which are hidden from the sea ... Had a talk with Admiral De Roebeck and Sir Ian. Got a good deal of information. We saw the effects of the shells that hit the Q.E. on the 18th* (March) *She was hit a good many times by field guns. Wonderfully lucky no one was hurt.*

April 13th. *... had a talk with Gen. Hunter-Weston* (Commander, Helles Landings) *and got a pretty complete account of how the operations are to be carried out ...*

April 15th. *Detail of landing, that is allotment of units to beaches and tows, has come out. The whole thing is made up by G.H.Q. and as they are dealing directly with O.C. ships I hear nothing about it except what I can pick up from my own C.O.'s. No doubt I will get it all in good time. What I can gather so far is that our Brigade is to be the covering force ... Also we are to land where I always wanted to land* (i.e. Helles).

April 16th. *Got further details as to landing from H.Q. and spent most of the morning making my plans accordingly which did not require much change from what I had already made. It is all working out exactly as I had hoped.* (Hare's diary does not record what was his attitude to the fighting qualities of the Turks) *In the afternoon went on board the collier* (the not yet famous SS *River Clyde,* destined to become an abiding image for all who landed later in the campaign at Helles) *which is to be run ashore with two of my battalions on board, Commander Unwin* (who was to be awarded the VC for his action at the landings on 25 April) *of H.M.S. Hussar, who is to run the show, took us round and showed us all his arrangements which are most complete. Other Naval Officers are a little sceptical about its success ...* (They were right about this but more through ill-fortune than weakness in the idea)

April 17th. *Breakfast at 7 in order to go and see practice landing from the collier. Unwin R.N. in command is very enthusiastic about his scheme. Doubt if the slight gain in time is worth the risk of losing two battalions if it goes wrong.* (I think Unwin deserves more than this; the alternative for those two battalions was to be rowed ashore while under fire!)

April 18th.   *Up early and went on board H.M.S. Dublin about 7.30 a.m. Gen. Hunter Weston and some of Staff, all Brigadiers and my C.O.'s were on board.   Steamed to Tenedos* (an island close to the peninsular).   *Saw the aerodrome on shore with several aeroplanes up.   Were transferred to the Swiftsure, Admiral Nicholson's flagship.   Started for Cape Helles about 12.30.   Lunch with Admiral.   All Captains of covering ships on board.   After lunch Hunter-Weston showed them all what the general plan of operations was to be.   All the sailors seem very keen to help us in every possible way, but they are not very confident about their own powers at indirect fire as they are accustomed only to shoot at what they can see.   As we got near Cape Helles we saw the Triumph and Majestic ... firing up the straits.   We steamed along the shore within about a mile and had a very good look.   We all went up into the tops with the General and as I had a telescope instead of field glasses I saw much better than last time.   They have made it very strong all round the extreme end but I don't see how they can hold it in the face of the bombardment.* (But they inflicted fearful casualties on most of the landing beaches - over confidence in the effect of bombardment seems to be a thread which is common to many battles.) *Here the sailors will be shooting at what they can see.   I do not anticipate much opposition to the actual landing except from long-range artillery fire.* (This was to be proved hopelessly wrong.   We are not told what evidence was available to support this convinced opinion; certainly no beach reconnaissance had been done.) *It will be in our further advance that we shall catch it.* (This was correct) *We had a few shots fired at us but none came very close ...*

April 19th.   *Spent most of morning seeing Company Commanders of the different regiments ... Am afraid one of my C.O.'s is going off his head or having a nervous break down.   Unpleasant business, but shall be glad to be rid of him ...*

April 20th.   *Blowing hard and got steadily worse during day.   Evidently no move will be possible so long as this lasts ... Had long talks with the General about operations of Covering Force which I am to command.   Everything satisfactory.   The Captain told me at dinner that he had orders to be ready to move tomorrow afternoon.   We are evidently going to move as soon as the weather improves.*

April 21st.   *Weather worse than ever ... Busy day preparing our Operation Orders and talking things over with various people.   Weather being slightly better all C.O.'s of Division succeeded in collecting on Andania for a conference.   We were to have moved today, but it has been put off 24 hours.*

April 22nd.   *Weather still doubtful and we don't know if we shall move tomorrow or not.   Got our Operation Orders completed and wrote letters.   Weather improving rapidly and quite calm by evening.*

April 23rd.   *Lovely morning, dead calm, fresh breeze got up afterwards but weather seems settled and we start this evening. During the afternoon the H.Q. 29th Division and various odds and ends of G.H.Q. came on board so we are all pretty crowded. Left for Tenedos at 6 p.m. accompanied by Ausonia and Caledonia taking the whole of the covering force and details for work on the beaches ...*

April 24th.   *Tenedos. Were to have started loading stores into lighters and shifting troops into battle ships, fleet sweepers, etc. first thing in the morning but it was blowing fresh and nothing could be done. Weather improved in afternoon and about 4 p.m. they got a move on ...*

It was a hopelessly over-optimistic plan, which took insufficient account of the effect of the enfilading fire from cliffs overlooking the beaches. In the early days of my growing awareness of Gallipoli, before I knew about the open boats and the cliffs, I had said to Len Chandler (from the Foley Arms) *"How come the casualties were so high on the first day?* The reply spoke it all:- *"Because they knew we were coming!"* And they did. No beach was large enough to allow a concentration of force.

The reader must recondition his thoughts about invasion. This was no D-Day style invasion of Normandy with its nervous but meticulous planning, and a brilliantly successful strategic deception. What was to be attempted had no precedent. Hamilton's job was to organise, in a matter of three weeks, the setting up of the largest amphibious operation ever attempted so far in the whole history of warfare. No invasion against beaches defended with modern weapons had ever been tried before. It was the cliffs that were the killer assisted by the barbed wire, some of it underwater. The beaches themselves had no comparison with Normany: they were perhaps only a few hundred yards wide overlooked by cliffs and hills. There were no cliffs on the Normandy beaches, except at Omaha beach - the only Normandy invasion beach where heavy losses were suffered.

Imagine, the invading soldiers being rowed into the attack, yes rowed. This is the scene where the 1st Battalion, Lancashire Fusiliers won their six VC's before breakfast. It seems scarcely credible that it should have been attempted. According to Moorehead:-

"Had they been able to get hold of some of the Navy's new armoured invasion boats it might have been a different story - but these were a closely guarded secret in the Admiralty at the time, and not even Kitchener was supposed to know anything about them." *

---

* These armoured landing craft, the first of their kind and the forerunner of the Normandy craft, were actually used for the Sulva Bay landings in August. The absence of them on 25 April cost massive casualties; the use of them at Sulva Bay was wasted!

What actually happened was that they used ship's boats strung together in tows, which were towed in to about 50 - 100 yards, then rowed the rest of the way. The casualties were dreadful. Brigadier-General Hare's diary describes a practice: *"After lunch a launch from the Implacable with some boats came and took ashore a company of Royal Fusiliers. They took 7 boats in one tow and could have done 8. Went quite a good pace but it was down wind. Self and staff went with them."* There is no reference in the diary to how dangerous is an approach by this method to a defended beach.

The whole system of the Turkish defence was based upon the principle that they must hold the hills so that they could overlook the enemy. Although the cliffs overlooking the landing beaches were taken (by weight of numbers and by sublime bravery) the most important hills were never taken. As Moorehead said:- *"It was not distance that counted on Gallipoli, nor even the number of soldiers or the guns of the Fleet; it was a simple issue of the hills. Later on fifty thousand men were to lose their lives around Chunuk Bair in establishing this fact."*

The Anzacs came close to taking Chunuk Bair. They were denied it by an inspired defensive manoeuvre by Mustafa Kemal, the commander who went on to lead Turkey into the modern world after the war. That the Anzacs did not take Chunuk Bair was another terrible 'If' of Gallipoli.

To some at the time it all seemed all too inevitable. The Rev. O. Creighton wrote in his diary on 22nd April: *"It seems a perfectly desperate undertaking. I can hardly expect to see many of my men alive again. My present feeling is that the whole thing has been bungled. The Navy should never have started the bombardment without the Army. Now there has been no bombardment for some weeks. Meanwhile the Turks, under German direction, have perfected their defences. The aerial reconnaissance reports acres of barbed wire, labyrinths of trenches, concealed guns, maxims and howitzers everywhere. The ground is mined. In fact everything conceivable has been done."* You couldn't have written it much better with the benefit of hindsight.

When the time came for Hamilton to think of reinforcements, he had his eye on the 42nd East Lancashire Division who were part of the force defending Egypt and which included the 1st/5th Battalion, the Lancashire Fusiliers.

This was the territorial battalion of which Private Ash was serving. His doom, and many of his pals were to be met at the third, and still unsuccessful battle for Krithia. These were the men who had joined the territorials before the war and who had volunteered, almost to a man, to renounce their 'home defence only' obligations. The 42nd East Lancashire Division was the first territorial division to arrive at Gallipoli. Private Ash left Bury in September 1914, his Division's job being to relieve regular troops by garrisoning Egypt. In the eight month's they had been in Egypt, their training for battle had continued. Hickey tells us that General Hamilton inspected the 42nd Division in March 1915 before he ever thought of asking for them as reinforcements. Hamilton wrote in his diary for 28 March: *"Inspected East Lancashire Division ... how I envied Maxwell* (Commander-in-Chief of forces in Egypt) *... What wouldn't I give to carry them off with me now. These Lancashire* (territorials) *... are eye-openers. How on earth have they managed to pick up the swank and devil-may-care of crack regulars ... no soldier need wish to see a finer lot?"* Just imagine if Sergeant-Major Ash had heard this spoken of his son's battalion. The reader can have no difficulty in understanding the pride that the town of Bury took in its men at arms!

According to Rhodes James, Brigadier-General Hare made a rallying call to his men on the eve of the invasion. Hare makes no reference to this event in his diary, which is curious; but someone must have written it down. It is epic stuff:-

"Fusiliers! Our Brigade is to have the honour to be the first to land and to cover the disembarkment of the rest of the division. Our task will be no easy one. Let us carry it through in a way worthy of the traditions of the distinguished regiments of which the Fusilier Brigade is composed ... in such a way that future historians may say of us, as Napier said of the Fusilier Brigade at Albuhera (during the Peninsular war) *- 'Nothing could stop that astonishing infantry'. "*

The officers and men were in high spirits as they prepared for battle. While in Edinburgh reference library I chanced upon a book *"Infantry uniforms"* by Robert and Christopher Wilkinson Latham and was able to discover how other ranks were equipped in 1915. Evidently they had the 1903 rig of a 5-pouch bandolier over the left shoulder and a waist-belt with two pouches at each side. On the left hip was the bayonet frog. A water bottle and a haversack were carried; on the back was a pack and rolled blanket. According to the Wilkinson Latham's, contemporary photographs of the Lancashire Fusiliers taken before the landings at Gallipoli (this would have been the 1st Battalion) show the men with the Lee-Enfield rifle with the 1888 pattern bayonet.

Brigadier-General Hare's diary entry for 25 April 1915, the day of the invasion, runs to over 1,500 words.

It is fascinating; here is some of it:-

April 25th.   *Got up at 3.30 a.m., breakfast at 4. Men all got a hot meal before getting into the boats. While it was getting light the tows were coming alongside and the men getting into the boats. The tows consisted of four boats towed by a launch, each boat took half a platoon i.e. two tows per company or 8 tows (32 boats) per battalion. As it began to get light about 4.30, we could see that we were lying not much more than a mile S.W. of Cape Tekke. The other ships were lying in a half circle round the end of the peninsula. Next to us to the East was the Euryalus, Admiral Wemys's flagship with the H.Q. and 3 companies Lancs. Fusiliers and the H.Q. 29th Division.*

The diary then gives the details of the landing plan for the 86th Brigade:-

'The morning was dead calm and clear but a bad light for us looking towards our landing place, as the sun was about to rise right behind it. There was some delay in the tows coming alongside so it was after 5.30 and the sun was up by the time we left the ship's side and it must have been about 5.45 by the time we landed. The bombardment had begun punctually at 5 but it did not have anything like the visible effect I had expected. (To the enormous cost of the first men ashore) *I had expected to see the whole end of the peninsula and especially the surroundings of the beaches one cloud of dust and smoke. As the long semicircle of tows steamed in towards the shore all was perfectly still except for the booming of the ships' guns - not a sign of life on shore and no one in boats uttering a sound. Our tows from the Implacable cut in just behind the tows from the Euryalus* with the rest of the battalion. The enemy at our beach never made a sign till the leading boats were close to the beach, 50 yards or so, then they fairly let rip with machine guns and musketry. Looking into the bay from where we were behind, we could see nothing. The sun was just above the cliff and the whole shore was a haze. We knew that they must be getting it hot from such heavy fire at close range but could not see very much except that a lot of men were falling in the water as they got out of the boats. The leading boats were beginning to return empty, evidently with men of their crews hit. We directed our boats towards the cliff just west of the beach, hoping to land under cover.*

We found the landing was gently sloping rock and got ashore all right, though many were hit in doing so. We started scrambling up the cliff, which was a steep earth slope with layers of rock here and there. It was not very steep but was difficult for a man in full kit to climb. There were no Turks on the front edge of the cliff, but were getting it pretty hot from the trenches on the east side of the mouth of the glen which formed the beach. When we got to the top we could see that the Lancashire Fusiliers were shoving on straight to their front up the glen but must have been losing frightfully from fire from the trenches on both sides. There was one trench just at the top of the cliff on the East side of the glen that was doing a lot of damage, but while we looked a shell from the Euryalus burst right in it and when the smoke cleared off no occupants could be seen and some Fusiliers got up the cliff and into it before it could be reoccupied. When we got to the top of the cliff we found an empty trench at the very edge. The occupants must have been shot out of it by the bombardment. We collected about a dozen Fusiliers there and an officer, about all who had reached the top, and sent them off to charge a trench which was only about 50 yards off, not facing us but flanking the glen leading up from the beach. Meanwhile I could hear no firing coming from beach X and concluding that the Royal Fusiliers had landed without opposition (which was correct) *I thought I would try and work round to meet them and bring them up to make a flank attack on the people who were opposing the Lancashire Fusiliers. The latter had made a certain amount of progress* (it

---

*   We have already heard of HMS *Euryalus*: see Chapter 3.

was wonderful that they made any*) *but I did not think they could possibly get far unsupported. I started with ... (others) and we were just above the cliff ... when we found ourselves within about 100 yards of a trench full of Turks. We started to drop over the top of the cliff as they opened fire. I felt a tremendous blow on my calf and just got over the edge of the cliff when I sat down. If the Turks had had the enterprise to come out of their trench and look for us they could have bagged the lot. I told ...* (the men with me) *to carry on what they were doing and I started to get back to the beach. I scrambled along the best I could and got about half way back when ...* (someone told me) *a stretcher was just coming. I was very glad of it as I had been feeling pretty lonely. There had been shooting going on just above me and one of the signallers had come back and told me they had been stopped by snipers. They had managed to get a message through. The stretcher-bearers turned up and put iodine into the wound and tied me up again. When I got to the beach a doctor again did me up and managed to stay the bleeding a little. I could see that my calf was in a pretty good mess but did not realise how bad it was till later. ...*
(a messenger) *told me that the Lancashire Fusiliers were getting on all right. They had certainly cleared their beach ... A lot of bullets were still flying about but they were not under direct fire. Boat loads of wounded were going off all the time and I was sent in one of them. They took me to the Euryalus and put me in the Admiral's cabin where my wound got properly dressed. It must have been between 8 and 9 when I got on board. Hunter Weston came down shortly to see me. He was very enthusiastic about the progress of events. So far the Royal Fusiliers had landed without opposition, so had the Marines and the Kings Own Scottish Borderers at beach Y. The Lancashire Fusiliers had got on well, a very fine performance ...*

Because of the order in which I made my discoveries of these events, the story of the bond between HMS *Euryalus* and the Lancashire Fusiliers has already been told in Chapter 3.

Brigadier-General Hare's survival of the landing was due to his being wounded**. The initiative he had shown in trying to link up with X Beach to hit West was brilliant. It was very bad luck that his successor was killed shortly afterwards. The continuation of Hare's leadership might have made the difference in exploiting quickly the X Beach success.

---

*   The Lancashire Fusiliers lost in the W Beach landing (i.e. *the Lancashire Landing*) 6 officers and 183 men killed, 4 officers and 279 men wounded, and 61 men missing, a total of 533 casualties. The Regiment won 6 VC's, 2 DSO's, 2 MC's and a DCM; they entered military legend. Source: Robert Rhodes James.

** He recovered from a flesh wound and returned to Gallipoli near the end and was involved in the evacuation from Sulva Bay. He was later promoted to Major-General and commanded the 54th Division in Egypt and Palestine from 1916 to 1919 in which year he was knighted. Retiring from the army in 1923, he died in 1952 at the age of 85.

In battles fought on Gallipoli death came from shellfire, machine gun or rifle fire or from the sniper's bullet; or death might come from disease or the neglect of wounds; but it would often come from the bayonet. It is difficult for a man who has no military training to come to terms with hand-to-hand fighting with a bayonet. Imagine, if you can, the need to get your thrust in first, to withdraw the blade only to make another deadly thrust, it time, if you were quick, to kill the next one of the enemy ready to kill you by the same means. You never hear soldiers speaking of this; of the thrust into the chest, of blood on the blade and yet, according to Hickey:-

"In the British army bayonet fighting was one of the sacred pillars of infantry training".

While in Edinburgh library I found a small booklet devoted to the subject of bayonet drill. It was an 1893 edition and Sergeant-Major Ash would be intimate with its contents. It was compiled by Sergeant-Major Gordon of the 2nd Battalion, Scots Guards who, as he helpfully notes, gives forty illustrations of the gruesome process!

The Western end of *Lancashire Landing*: the defended cliffs were assaulted from open boats. Brigadier-General Hare was wounded on the high ground. Author's photo, 2002.

There were over 42,000 Commonwealth soldiers and sailors who died at Gallipoli or of their wounds elsewhere*. Of these, 29,000 were British, 8,000 Australian, 3,000 New Zealand and 2,000 Indian. The French lost about 10,000. The Turkish losses are vague. Rhodes James thinks the official estimate of 80,000 dead is a considerable under estimate. The great majority of soldiers who died on Gallipoli have no known grave. These losses, though frightful, are very small compared with the mass destruction of life on the Western Front in France; the losses at Gallipoli were suffered in defeat for the Allies.

During my research for this book I came across a book by H.G. Wells (the English novelist, social theorist and prophet) called *"Little Wars; a game for boys"*. On dipping into it, I realised it was a sort of manual to help boys to play *"toy soldiers"*. In it are written these words which I stumbled upon:-

"I have never yet met in little battle (i.e. playing at toy soldiers) *any military gentleman, any captain, major, colonel, general or lieutenant commander, who did not presently get into difficulties and confusion among even the elementary rules of the battle. You only have to play at Little Wars three or four times to realise what a blundering thing Great War must be.*
Great War is at present, I am convinced, not only the most expensive game in the universe, but it is a game out of all proportion. Not only are the masses of men and material and suffering and inconvenience too monstrously big for reason, but the available heads we have for it, are too small. That, I think, is the most pacific realisation conceivable, and Little War brings you to it as nothing else but Great War can do."

If this had been written in the knowledge of the outrages of Gallipoli, the Somme and Verdun, one could have done nothing but agree. H.G. Wells wrote the words in 1913; an enduring monument to his prescience.

A.J.P. Taylor, the historian looked back. Writing in 1965 of the failed Dieppe raid in August 1942, he explains that initially, the commander (Montgomery) had insisted on air cover and a heavy naval bombardment.

"Then the RAF announced it had no aeroplanes to spare, and the Admiralty refused to supply any big ships. Montgomery, fortunately for his reputation, left for the Middle East. The plans went on of their own momentum, and the raid was undertaken despite the lack of all the conditions which had been laid down for its success." It was Gallipoli once more: *"improvised muddle again brought discreditable failure."*

There was failure too at Anzio in January 1944. The ingenious plan, inspired again by Churchill, was to land in the rear of the Germans, who were holding up the Allies badly at Casino, and so cut them off and take Rome. According to Taylor:-

---

* The source of the Commonwealth statistics is research done by Patrick Gareipy of the Gallipoli Association.

"The American commander was concerned to establish his position instead of rushing forward. Alexander (the theatre commander) *was too courteous to push him on, just like Hamilton at Gallipoli ..."* It was indeed Gallipoli all over again: *"inspired by the same man and with the the same result."* * Normandy, in June 1944, was different: in that case the political and military imperatives came together in an immaculate synchronisation !

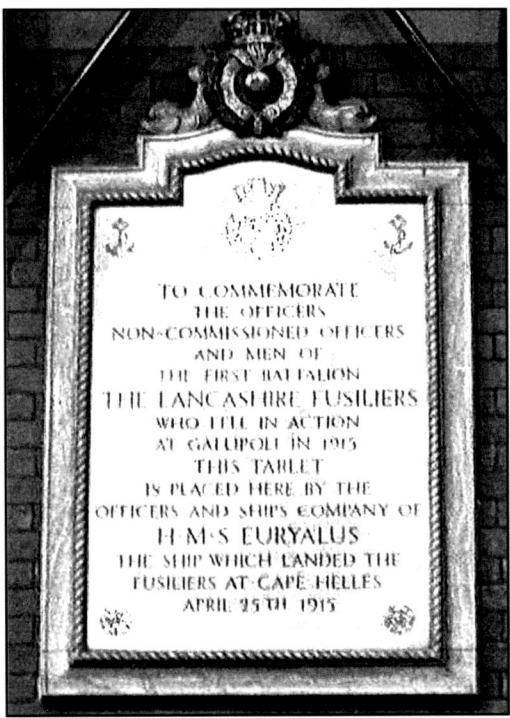

The officers and men of *HMS Euryalus* dedicated this plaque in Bury Parish Church to the men of the 1st Battalion, Lancashire Fusiliers who landed at Cape Helles from *Euryalus's* cutters.

---

* To criticise Churchill over the lost opportunities at Anzio requires an absolution from fault in the way Generals conducted themselves after the invasion had first succeeded.

Chapter 10

Serendipity

When I was in Bury during the visit in which I discovered the film of Sergeant-Major Ash's funeral, an idea began to impress itself into my mind. Colour-Sergeant Hickie (not to be confused with Major Michael Hickey, author of '*Gallipoli*'), had come into the story and I was intrigued to establish that both men were given clocks on their retirement on the same day. I had a vision of a pair of identical clocks: to re-unite these clocks became an idea on which I gradually focused. This caused a few wry smiles among those to whom I mentioned it; but I wasn't put off. I now had the hang of the Public Record Office in Kew and I could start my researching by looking up the attestation and discharge papers of Colour-Sergeant Hickie. Somewhere out there, I surmised, there was a great grandson with another handsome timepiece dedicated to another man who had given faithful service to the 1st Volunteer Battalion, the Lancashire Fusiliers.

In Kew I discovered that Colour-Sergeant Henry Hickie served with the Lancashire Fusiliers for 31 years, having joined in 1876, the year after Sergeant-Major Ash joined the Scots Guards. He and his wife had nine children, five of whom were boys. His discharge papers noted his intended place of residence to be 38 Brierly Street, Heywood, and the town near Bury where Hickie served with

Members of the Lancashire Fusilier Battalions file into church for Sergeant-Major Ash's funeral;   the moustached Sergeant passing the policeman is Colour-Sergeant Hickie, the man to whom was presented a *handsome timepiece* on the same occasion in 1907 as Sergeant-Major Ash, when they both retired from the Volunteer Battalion of the Lancashire Fusiliers. Hickie, like Ash, rejoined the Regiment on the outbreak of war in 1914. Hickie survived into old age.

(Courtesy, North West Film Archive at Manchester Metropolitan University)

the 1st Volunteer Battalion. This, I thought, would be the basis of some research. It was an uncommon name; I had a town and, happily, there were five male children able to hand the name down. This would put me at considerable advantage over researching the Ash's descendants in which there were no surviving males: I knew that for a fact from my grandmother. I had accounted for one of his sons, George Vivian, who died at Gallipoli, but Victor John had disappeared with no trace; there is no evidence that he served in the Army*: he is not on the 'Soldiers Died' CD Rom; he was at the Sergeant-Major's funeral in 1915 but there was no reference to him having a wife. My mother, who was born in 1910, had never made any reference to him. So, there was no line of Ash for me to follow up. The Hickies would be different, I reasoned.

It didn't matter: 'Seek and ye shall find' is a very pleasant biblical suggestion. Certainly, one is very unlikely to find what is not being sought. In this case serendipity came to my aid very promptly. I mentioned to Tony Sprason, the Custodian at the Lancashire Fusiliers Museum that I was going to try to trace Colour-Sergeant Hickie's clock. *"Oh"*, he said, *"His grandson's been in"*. Evidently, Major John Hickie MBE had been to the Museum researching his man in the same way I had with mine.

I wrote to Major Hickie. Can you imagine receiving a letter such as the one I wrote? This is what I said:-

"This letter will arrive with you out of the blue; nonetheless I hope it will be fully as agreeable to you as it is unexpected.

Sergeant-Major Ash and Colour-Sergeant Hickie served together in the 1st Volunteer Battalion, Lancashire Fusiliers until 1907. I suspect they were good friends; without doubt Henry Hickie attended Sergeant-Major Ash's funeral in 1915. Sergeant-Major Ash was my great-grandfather ...

In the Lancashire Fusiliers Annual of 1907 are written the following words which you may have seen:

'Sergeant-Major Ash and Colour-Sergeant Hickie have now left us. The officers presented each of them with a handsome timepiece as a memento of faithful service rendered over many years.'

As I write these words the Sergeant-Major's clock ticks on. It has been in his family's hands ever since his death. Do you have Colour-Sergeant Hickie's clock?

I am currently writing a book about Sergeant-Major Ash, his clock and his soldier son(s). I would like to include something about Colour-Sergeant Hickie and his clock.

When you have collected yourself from this perhaps remarkable turn of events I

---

* Because of *'the burnt records'* this cannot be a secure conclusion.

would be most pleased to hear from you."

As I posted the letter I found it very difficult to imagine what impact it might have. I could not work out what the reaction would be, other than surprise bordering on shock. This is what Major Hickie wrote back:

"Thank you very much indeed for your letter, which as you said came 'straight out of the blue' ... I am enclosing a copy of a small family history booklet that I have done on the service of Henry Hickie ... In fact Henry Hickie was my grandfather although he died before I was born in June 1934. My father was born in December 1889 when Henry was 35 and was the fourth of nine children, two of whom died young. My father was 45 when I was born and I am an only child, my father dying in 1939 when I was aged 4.

As you can see from my booklet I was aware of Sergeant-Major Ash and of the presentation of the 'handsome timepiece'. Of Henry Hickie's family all his children are now dead. Of his grandchildren I am only aware of myself and three others all of whom I am in contact with, all four of us coming from different children of Henry and living in different parts of the country.

I am sorry to say that I do not think that ... (the clock) *exists any more ...* (Here Major Hickie speculates on a distant memory a cousin has of a clock, long disappeared, but whose description bears no similarity to Sergeant-Major Ash's clock). *Equally so the clock may simply have died of its own accord in the interim years. There is one final possibility and that is that it found its way to Henry Hickie's youngest son ...* (In due course Major Hickie cleared this possibility).

Incidentally Henry Hickie's sons all served in the Lancashire Fusiliers in WW1 with the exception of my father who for some reason or other served in the 15th (London Welsh) Battalion of the Royal Welsh Fusiliers! ... I was in the Artillery from 1953 -1989, and my eldest son also went into the Gunners. My second son first qualified as a Radiographer and then went into the Medical Corps. So between us four generations of the Hickie family served in the army !! ...

Anyway once again thank you very much indeed for your letter. I am sorry that I cannot progress your clock story ... "

The history of the Hickie family was evidently quite different from that of the Ash family. All of Colour-Sergeant Hickie's sons survived the war, and flourished, and then the family saw service in the Second World War. It has branches all over the place. I have no Ash family but in compensation I do have his *"handsome timepiece"*, to which, as will be plain to the reader, I have acquired a bond the strength of which would defy any force I could imagine.

Before long, I received another letter from Major Hickie. This is what he said:-

"My cousin Trevor has now returned from the States ... Sadly he does not have the Hickie

'timepiece' and has no knowledge of it whatsoever. He even wondered if it was identical or similar to yours. In my opinion it would have been the same. In those days senior ranks retiring from the army would have had no choice in whatever gift their officers chose to present them with. Even in my day one didn't have a choice ! When Mary and I got married the traditional wedding present was a silver cigarette box suitably inscribed. The only difference between say 1963 and 1923 say, was that the box got smaller !!! Again in my day the traditional leaving present from a Regiment was a good solid pewter tankard. Before the war they were silver tankards and by the time I left the army they were really quite inferior tankards! In my son's days even tankards were out and the Regimental plaque was in! All a question of money, and the 'handsome timepieces' would not have been cheap."

In later correspondence, after checking with all the various branches of the Hickie family, which naturally took some time, Major Hickie had to confirm that there was definitely no trace of Colour-Sergeant Hickie's clock. Strange: disappointing too, but it made Sergeant-Major Ash's clock an even bigger treasure. It was now into the fourth generation of owners. I discerned that it ticked even more proudly now and I was even more proud of it.

No clock, then, for Henry Hickie's descendants. It seemed rather a shame to have stirred up the issue from their point of view. It may have made me feel better about my clock but it was a little self-centred. In due course I was able to make amends, through serendipity, in splendid style.

As soon as it arrived, two months earlier, I glanced quickly at Major Hickie's monograph *"The Military career of Henry Hickie"*. Henry Hickie survived until 1932, dying in a nursing home at the age of 78. His obituary relates that: *"In 1888 he was promoted Colour-Sergeant Instructor for the 1st Volunteer Battalion of the Lancashire Fusiliers at Bury ..."* Sergeant-Major Ash joined the battalion in 1894 and, therefore, because they were serving together in 1915, they must have known each other for over 20 years. His funeral, like Sergeant-Major Ash's was also a military one, notwithstanding the fact that he had left the army in 1918, some fourteen years before he died.

"The cortege was headed by a firing party of the 5th Battalion, Lancashire Fusiliers ... The coffin was draped with the Union Jack, on which were (the) *deceased's Busby and belt. He was burred in his scarlet coat and dark trousers - the uniform worn before the khaki uniform was adopted. A large crowd of people witnessed the funeral* (just like Sergeant-Major Ash) *... three volleys were fired and a bugle sounded 'the last post' followed by the 'Reveille'."*

As I continued turning the pages I was struck by déja vu. There, in print was:-

"Sergeant-Major Ash and Colour-Sergeant Hickie have now left us. The officers presented each of them with a handsome timepiece as a memento of faithful service rendered for many years."

So, the pair of them, friends I suspect for 20 years, both left the Lancashire Fusiliers on the same day, both were given a clock, both joined up again in 1914 and both had their stories told 90 years later. Amazing.

I have never written fiction. I am not sure I have sufficient imagination to make up stories. I couldn't have made up the story told in this book. I defy any reader to guess the next, and final, discoveries. I have already related how I discovered the film of Sergeant-Major Ash's funeral. I was showing it to Len Chandler one day when I said *"Have a look at this, but before you do, look at this photo of Colour-Sergeant Hickie"*. As we watched the film, Len had no hesitation in identifying the man in the photo as one of the soldiers filing into church at the funeral. He had confirmed what I had already thought.

The problem now was what to do with this belief that Colour-Sergeant Hickie was in the 1915 newsreel film in relation to Major Hickie, his grandson. It was clear that he knew nothing of the film, even though he knew of Sergeant-Major Ash, for there was no mention of it in the research he had done.

I was nervous of claiming a recognition if it turned out to be wrong. I had already stirred up the missing clock saga and I had no wish to set a new hare running. I decided to telephone Major Hickie and to discuss it with him. We had a thoroughly enjoyable thirty-five minute conversation. He decided to get his own copy of the film from the North West Film Archive. A month later I had another letter from Major Hickie:

... In the post today I received from the North West Film Archive my copy of Sergeant-Major Ash's funeral. What a tremendous insight into life in 1915 and how wonderful for you to have on record your great grandfather's funeral. It is certainly something to be kept, treasured and handed down.

Both Mary and I think that the film does capture my grandfather, Colour-Sergeant Henry Hickie. We think that he appears after the column of two's of younger soldiers, in the party of NCO's, nearest to the camera and second from the end before the group of officers.

The person in question is certainly a Colour-Sergeant, build and hair seem about right, as does the age. He also certainly has the 'swagger' of a regular army senior NCO!

Today I spoke to my cousin ... who remembers her grandfather although she was only seven when he died. She said that he was well built but not fat and always held himself very erect which fits the picture. She also said that his hair was light with a gingerish tinge and a good head of hair and full moustache. All these also match.

So what more can I say ? Without you getting in contact I would never have known of the existence of this piece of film. Again, and really only with the agreement of my elder cousins, we will have a wonderful cameo of my grandfather to hand down to future generations ..."

Not many weeks later I had another letter from Major Hickie:-

Just a very brief note to give you an update on the Hickie side of the video on Sergeant-Major Ash's funeral.

I got the video back from my cousin Zoe who was rising twelve when my grandfather died, lived next door to him and saw him nearly every day. I have spoken on the phone to her and she is positive that the man in question is our grandfather Henry Hickie

So here we have it. Positive identification had been made of the man by a grand-daughter who knew him intimately. This was very satisfying but was not the end of surprises.

However, (Major Hickie's letter continued) *there is more to it than that. She is also fairly certain that Henry's eldest son, Harry, is also on the video and she recognised him straight away! She says that he is on the far side from the camera, tall, slim and with a moustache. He appears in the group of soldiers marching in twos and is amongst the first of those to remove his head dress. He is the one who appears to be 'changing step' as he wheels to the right and off camera! So that is absolutely tremendous.*

No one seems to have a photograph of 'Uncle Harry' so I had no idea what he looked like. he had joined the Lancashire Fusiliers and ended the war as an RSM, reputedly with an MC, but I have not been able to find a record of this. He continued in the army after the war and according to Zoe would come home on leave, as they did in those days, in his uniform. Later in the 1930's he was supposed to have gone down to the Battersea area and no one knows what happened to him after that. I once tried writing to all the Hickies at Battersea but to no avail!

Back to the video, I don't know if I told you but Mary always laughs when she watches it because she says that I walk exactly like Henry Hickie !! I hope that all goes well with your visit up to Lancashire and for the presentation of the painting of Sergeant-Major Ash. If you ever take a photograph of the painting I would love to have a copy.

Once again many thanks, and I will keep you informed if I discover anything new."

This was, indeed, a most unexpected and happy outcome of a four-month correspondence, which had come about through serendipity. I wrote back:-

"I was delighted to have your letter of 25 October. If it seems a long while before I have replied, this is simply that I wanted to absorb the enormity of the news in your letter.

I had always been a little uncomfortable about having stirred up the story of Colour-Sergeant Hickie's 'handsome timepiece' only to have had to force you to confront the fact

141

that it had disappeared in unknown circumstances. After you had reached the conclusion, following a check with all the various branches of his family, I felt a little selfish when the 'nil return' had to be accepted. It was a pity to remind you all of the former existence of the clock and then for me to stand aside while you had to park the memory away; clearly Henry Hickie's clock has gone in circumstances which cannot now be discovered. I am reminded of my great uncle Victor John Ash. He has disappeared. I wondered when I started this business whether he had died in the Great War but he is not on the list! It is conceivable the records are not accurate but I am at a loss to know what became of him; a bit like Henry's clock.

Having set a hare running in relation to Henry's clock, you may imagine how thrilled I am to hear your cousin Zoe's positive identification of Henry on the film of Sergeant-Major Ash's funeral. That she knew him from her first moments of awareness to when she was nearly 12 gives an indisputable provenance to the identification.

Turning back to your letter, I could scarcely believe it when I read on to discover the next revelation. So Uncle Harry has turned up now that you now have an 86-year old film! Amazing ! You couldn't make this up could you? I am so pleased for all your film record of these men in their uniform. By the way, if Harry won an MC, there will be a record of it at Kew.

I am going back to Bury tomorrow. I have a date with the Mayor to be presented with the portrait of Sergeant-Major Ash with the artist, Mark Adams. The Bury Times will be there. You will indeed get a photo of the portrait.

I am staying on in Bury for the Remembrance Day service in Bury Parish Church. I will be wearing my Gallipoli Association tie. I will be interested to discern how the event is observed in Bury now that so much time has passed and the Lancashire Fusiliers no longer have their name. I am minded to go back to Bury next April for Gallipoli Sunday. Now that I know I have family connections I feel I have been admitted to a brotherhood. If I am in a brotherhood, I must be about the last one to join it!

Well, I will close now with one final thought. If the word 'serendipity' did not exist, we would have had to invent it. How else can we describe the circumstances in which we have uncovered these treasures together in the last few months?"

The story was coming to an end, at least for the time being. I resolved quite early in the story, almost immediately that I discovered that Private George Vivian Ash died at Gallipoli that I was going to visit the battlefields. No power could stop me; that is for the future and I intend to go with Colonel Michael Hickey (and a party from the Gallipoli Association). There is no writer on the Gallipoli campaign who does not remark on its pulling power for anyone with an interest in battles or a family connection. I have both: I am going; that will be another story.

In the meanwhile, I had as already recounted, through serendipity, met an artist at the Lancashire Fusiliers Museum. I had commissioned him to paint a portrait of Sergeant-Major Ash. I made a plan to pick up the picture, and the one of Private Ash which I had also commissioned from a *Bury Times* photo, over the week-end of Remembrance Sunday so that I could attend the parade and church service. I also resolved to introduce this story to the Mayor of Bury in the hope that he would be willing to conduct a presentation of the portrait of the Sergeant-Major as a promotion of the Lancashire Fusiliers Museum. I wrote to His Worship The Mayor telling him:

"... this is a human interest story which celebrates Bury and the Lancashire Fusiliers. You may care to embrace this story and, by presenting a new portrait of Sergeant-Major Ash by a local artist, help to promote Bury and the Fusilier's Museum at Bolton Road, Bury.

Just a few months ago I inherited a clock ... all I knew of the Sergeant-Major was the inscription on the clock and a few memories of the esteem in which he was held by my mother's family: all my mother's family have died out and I am in touch with none of the Sergeant-Majors descendants, other than my brother.

So, in March, the only hard facts that I had were the inscription on the clock ...When I first knew the clock I was a child visiting my grandparents, Harry and Cissie Barlow, in the 1940's and 1950's, who were then living in Grosvenor Street, Bury, where it stood proudly in their front parlour.

After I inherited the clock I became intrigued by the inscription on it and uncomfortable with my ignorance of the man whose clock it was, and his life. I decided to investigate. What I have discovered is as astonishing as it was unexpected. My sources have been the Lancashire Fusiliers Museum; the Public Record Office, Kew; the Family Records Centre, London; the Commonwealth War Graves Commission; the archives of the Bury Times and the North West Film Archive of Manchester Metropolitan University.

This is a catalogue of discoveries about Sergeant-Major Ash:-

* He left his Dorset home in 1875, where he was a farm labourer, at the age of 17 to join up.
* He served over 31 years in the Army in successively the Scots Guards, the Royal Fusiliers and the Lancashire Fusiliers until he retired in 1907.
* He served in the Egyptian Campaign of 1882 where he earned the Egyptian Star and the Khedive's Medal; he was later to be awarded good conduct and long service medals.
* He took up as licensee of successively the Grey Mare Hotel, formerly in Haymarket Street/Knowsley Street, Bury and the Nob Inn, Little Lever.
* On war breaking out in 1914 he joined up again, in the 5th Reserve Battalion, Lancashire Fusiliers.
* He died in service of a heart attack at home on 8 March 1915.
* His military funeral in Bury Parish Church was attended by thousands.

* He has a Commonwealth War Grave headstone to his grave in Manchester Road Cemetery, Bury;
* Twelve weeks later, his eldest son, Private George Vivian Ash died in Gallipoli, serving with the 1st/5th Battalion, Lancashire Fusiliers.

In its editorial on 13 March 1915 the Bury Times said: *"An honourable career came to an end with the death of Sergeant-Major Ash on Monday (8 March 1915). ...*

The Sergeant-Major was of fine presence - a typical Guardsman in appearance, and in every respect a smart and able soldier. He had the true soldier's respect for the King's Commission, and nothing could exceed the promptness with which he accorded it the full measure of honour. He was ever a courteous and obliging Sergeant-Major ... His return to military duties after more than seven years of retirement was probably in accordance with his own wishes as it undoubtedly was in accordance with his sense of duty ... The scene at his funeral ... was ... one such as we seldom witness even at interments at which full military honours are accorded.

Perhaps the most stunning part of the story is that his funeral was filmed as a news-reel and shown in the Art Picture House, Knowsley Street, Bury during the week after his funeral. Thanks to the North West Film Archive, I have a copy of that film. Imagine: in March this year all I knew was the inscription on the clock!

When I started my research I had no visual image of Sergeant-Major Ash. I have commissioned a local artist, Mark Adams, to paint his portrait in his full dress uniform drawn from a photo I found in the Bury Times archive. Would you be willing to present the picture to me ?

The Mayor, Councillor Paul Nesbit, graciously consented to make the presentation in the presence of Colonel Brian Gorski MBE and Captain John O'Grady (Ret'd) of the Royal Regiment of Fusiliers. This was a generous gesture, which may be used to illustrate that, at least for formal occasions, the military culture of Bury is still alive. This was further illustrated at the service on Remembrance Sunday. In his prologue to the service inside Bury Parish Church, the Rector, The Reverend John Finlon said:-

"The life we lead is in large part an inheritance from the past. The thoughts we think and the language that expresses them; our customs and traditions; the laws which protect us; our towns, our cities and our institutions; all have been bequeathed to us by our forebears for us to enjoy and, in our turn, to pass on to those who follow us. But the greatest of these legacies is the priceless gift of freedom. A treasury of hope won at great cost by those who fought to curb the power of tyrants, repel invaders and defend the right of their countrymen and women to live in liberty, with justice and with dignity.

We are gathered here today to acknowledge before God our great debt to those who laid down their lives in this noble cause: to remember them with pride and thanksgiving and to pray that we may prove ourselves worthy of their sacrifice.

We remember that to every generation the choice is given either to squander or to conserve the inheritance of the past, either to seek the common good or to forsake it in pursuit of selfish ends.

And we recognise that we have not always deserved our heritage. Price, selfishness, bitterness and greed still hold sway among us. We have been careless of our responsibility to those who will follow us, as well as in our accountability to Almighty God.

So let us confess to God the sins and the shortcomings of the world, of which we are part; its pride, its selfishness, its greed, its evil divisions and hatreds.

Let us confess our share in what is wrong, and our failure to seek and establish that peace which God wills for his children."

This is no platitudinous cant! If anyone wanted to challenge it, I don't know how it would be done. As a member of that lucky generation which has fought no wars; has never been conscripted or from which no voluntary military service has been sought I exalt the freedom that has been won for us; a freedom of spirit enjoyed alongside a lifetime of freedom from want. In his sermon the Reverend Finlon made his probably twice-yearly reference to Gallipoli. If it is *de rigueur* to speak its name, the context of the reference made it seem perfectly normal to a man who was, for the first time in his life remembering a death in Gallipoli, seated as he was with scores of others who had remembered every year of their lives.

The next day, after the Service, I went to the Sergeant-Major's grave in order to put on it a poppy. I was astonished to discover on the grave a pot of fresh flowers, presumably put there the previous day, 11 November. Moreover, on the plastic envelope in which I had left my message just two month's earlier was pinned a poppy. This proved a number of things. First, it proved that someone was caring for an eighty-six year old grave and that, whoever that person was knew of my existence and my interest in the grave. I felt sure that someone would get in touch with me but, curiously no one has. For the present this mystery remains unsolved.

However, I drove south with my portraits of father and son. Both had been painted from contemporary photographs. The one of Private George Vivian Ash presented no great difficulties, with a higher quality reproduction in the original photo, but also, because he was dressed in his 1914 khaki, the artist only needed to be shown the insignia and buttons of the uniform to be able to produce a picture which looks as if it might have been painted while he was on embarkation leave. The portrait of the Sergeant-Major was a much more difficult matter. The reproduction from the 1915 *Bury Times* photograph was not at all good. This was not just because it was a black and white image of the man in his full dress uniform with its scarlet tunic. It was because the quality of the picture was inherently inferior. The Lancashire Fusiliers Museum came up trumps by being able to show the artist, Mark Adams, full size models of the uniform and examples of all the insignia and other detail, which was on the photo but not so obviously that any detail could be discerned. This lucky help was most dramatically illustrated by the artist's work on the Sergeant-Major's medals. In the photo he was working on, the medals had been cut off by the lower margin. The custodian, Tony Sprason, found actual examples of the medals, which the artist was able to paint from the real images.

As I drove south feeling very proud of the portraits of my grandmother's father and her brother, there was only one more thread to this tale before bringing it to a close. The story had grown out of conversations in the Foley Arms in Claygate. There had now grown up in that pub a sub-branch of the Gallipoli Association and my next task was to put on display my portraits in the pub and to have an official branch meeting. This duly took place and the portraits had their showing amongst all those regulars who had participated in the evolution of this story; a story which had only begun eight months earlier.

It seemed appropriate to close this account where it started. Being close to Remembrance Sunday the work of the war poets was being aired. This story has been an account of the antithesis of remembering; it is an account of how a conspiracy to forget was overcome.

I was, therefore, particularly intrigued by how ironic was the exhortation in the March 1919 poem of Siegfried Sasoon which he called *'Aftermath'*.

Do you remember the nights you watched and wired and dug and piled
sandbags on the parapets ?
Do you remember the rats; and the stench
of corpses rotting in front of the front-line trench -
And dawn coming, dirty-white, and chill with a hopeless rain?
Do you ever stop to ask, 'Is it all going to happen again?'

Do you remember that hour of din before the attack -
And the anger, the blind compassion that seized and shook you then
As you peered at the doomed and haggard faces of your men?
Do you remember the stretcher-cases lurching back
With dying eyes and lolling heads?

Have you forgotten yet? ...
Look up, and swear by the green of the spring that you'll never forget.

These are powerful words and worthy of a few moments of quiet reflection for their own sake.

But I must crave a mental contortion for I am certain that my grandmother did her best not to remember, but to forget, and not only to forget but also to shield me and my brother from the knowledge. She didn't tell me anything, but I found out; I found out in the end. She won't mind: she will be proud that the truth has come out. Won't she be thrilled and amazed when she finds out that:

"It all started with a clock !"

The story of how the story of 'Where is Gallipoli?' was published in the Bury Times on 1st January 2002.

Chapter 11

Sequel

When I came back from the portrait presentation in Bury, I finished writing. All that the reader has read so far was written in 2001. That it has taken me three more years to bring the story to print begs the sequel to the story to be told. In September 2003 David Hare, my companion from the Foley Arms and a part of the genesis of the story died bravely from cancer. I wrote a piece for the Gallipolian: No. 103, Winter 2003/2004, about the contribution that his grand father had made at *Lancashire Landing.* I resolved that if I were to bring my story of the clock out, the book would be dedicated to David Hare.

My reticence in doing anything with the 2001 manuscript was partly because other projects intervened in my life, but it was also to do with the loose ends that had been left in the story. The mystery of the tributes left on the grave - the missing clock, the fact that no trace had been found of Victor nor baby Fred - all these missing links were getting in the way of a good story. But my interest was aroused by the visit of the *"handsome timepiece"* to the BBC's *Antiques Roadshow !*

The roadshow appeared at a local venue in May 2004, and I decided to take it along. It did not appear on TV, but an expert appraisal of it was given. The reader will recall that my surmise had been that two identical clocks had been presented to Sergeant-Major Ash and Colour-Sergeant Hickie, although some doubt had been thrown on this by the fragmentary recall of members of the Hickie family. There was no atom of doubt in the expert's view that the clock was much earlier than 1907 when it was given to George Ash. It was apparently a type of clock that had evolved from black mourning clocks, which were popular from the time of Queen Victoria's bereavement in 1861. Such clocks passed out of fashion and developed 20 to 30 years later into more attractive, one might say more 'handsome' pieces, which, while still made of black marble, they were brighter than those somewhat morbid pieces from which they had evolved. This was fascinating stuff: it meant that the clock was from the mid 1880's and that the clock was, therefore, second-hand when it was given to George Ash in 1907 - it also meant that Hickie's clock would have been different, and that there never were two identical clocks to be traced! The expert also observed that the 120-year old clock, never having been restored in its appearance, would benefit from the black marble being made more black, and the gilt being made more gold! The *handsome timepiece* did not come home from the *Antiques Roadshow:* it went straight to restoration from which it has now emerged and it now stands even more proudly than it did before. This experience quickened my resolve to tell the clock's secrets.

In the meanwhile after putting my pen down in 2001, I was not idle in trying trace Victor and baby Fred, but to no avail. I exhausted every means that I knew in tracing techniques from official records with no result. I even tried a non-official method. I wrote to every 'Ash' in the Greater Manchester phone book - about 30 of them. I received a very high response - but no news. Although I had to give up, the lack of any trace was consistent with what I remember my grand-mother telling me: no male members of the Ash family survived the Great War !

There was still the mystery of the Sergeant-Major's grave: who was tending it? Time was needed for a response to my calling card on his Commonwealth War Graves Commission headstone: none has come ! The *Bury Times* helped me by doing a feature on the story of the clock and my quest to discover its secrets and the missing links. The newspaper published a double page feature on the story, but with no result - bar one serendipitous sequel. The reader will recall my visits to 36 Grosvenor Street to visit my grandparents and where I had first become acquainted with the *'handsome timepiece'* - by an extraordinary coincidence that house is now owned by one of Terry Morgan's colleagues at the *Bury Times*, Mr. Steve Shimmin. When I was in Bury later for Gallipoli Sunday I arranged to revisit the house by courtesy of Mr. and Mrs. Shimmin, nearly 50 years after I had last been there. It was an extraordinary experience: many features of the house were recognisable, others not. I went into the *parlour,* the home of the *'handsome timepiece'* and in my mind I could both see it and hear it in its old familiar place.

In the intervening time I was able to follow up the *Euryalus* link with the Lancashire Fusiliers. I traced two model cutters cast in silver, which replicate the open boats in which the 1st Battalion landed at Helles: one in the Tower of London, the other in the officer's mess at North Luffenham.

The final matter to recall in this sequel is my visit to Gallipoli in May 2002 with a group from the Gallipoli Association led by Colonel Michael Hickey. It is understandable that men and women should stumble with their emotions on such ruinous battlefield sites, and many did. I went to Krithia, as near as could be guessed to the place where George Vivian Ash fell and felt chilled by the thought of a battle fought with the bayonet. Later we were taken to a cemetery near the battle-site where, on my own in a quiet corner of the immaculate space, I had an experience that is difficult to describe. The chums that I met on the trip have expressed surprise that I do not want to go back to Gallipoli, as many do - I have never been able to explain properly my reasons. There must, I think, be a genetic reason which is handed down by my grandmother: a desire to cover grief.

In that quiet corner of a cemetery in Gallipoli - a place where Private George Vivian Ash died but has no grave - I found the grave of a man from Bury; a man from the 1st/5th Battalion, Lancashire Fusiliers; the 'Saturday Night Soldiers' - the Territorials; the grave of a man who lived and worked in Bury; a man who would certainly have known Vivian; a man who may have been Vivian's friend, but a man who certainly died with him. As I looked at this grave of a stranger to me but of a man who died on the same day in the same battle and from the same town as Private George Ash, the man to whom I had attributed the intonation

'Where *is* Gallipoli ? '

I was overcome. I wept. I wept for my grandmother; I wept 60 years of tears for Vivian; for you see before I inherited the clock, I didn't know. But now the secrets of the clock had been largely revealed. I wept as a mother would weep for her son; I wept for Bury. No: I don't want to go back to Gallipoli! The genes of my grandmother are calling: they are saying:-

"The grief is all too much to bear: close now".

A group photo of the May 2002 Gallipoli Association visit to the peninsular, with the guide, Colonel Michael Hickey in the centre, at the Helles Memorial where Private George Vivian Ash is remembered.

151

In December 2001, after a presentation in the Mayor's parlour attended by the artist, Mark Adams, the author was photographed with Colonel Brian Gorsky, Royal Regiment of Fusiliers (left) and Captain John O' Grady.

On 4 December 2001, at the Foley Arms, Claygate, the newly painted portraits of George Ash and Vivian Ash (by Mark Adams) were displayed. Here they are with the author (left), with David Hare (died 2003) , grandson of Sir Steuart Hare, Commander of the Fusilier Brigade at Gallipoli, and Len Chandler, whose interest in Gallipoli prompted the investigation into the clock's secrets.   (Author's photo)

INDEX